Practicing Leadership

Practicing Leadership

Alan S. Gutterman

BEP BUSINESS EXPERT PRESS

Practicing Leadership

Copyright © Business Expert Press, LLC, 2019.

First published in 2019 by
Business Expert Press, LLC
222 East 46th Street, New York, NY 10017
www.businessexpertpress.com

ISBN-13: 978-1-94999-121-5 (paperback)
ISBN-13: 978-1-94999-122-2 (e-book)

Business Expert Press Human Resource Management and Organizational Behavior Collection

Collection ISSN: 1946-5637 (print)
Collection ISSN: 1946-5645 (electronic)

Cover and interior design by Exeter Premedia Services Private Ltd., Chennai, India

First edition: 2019

10 9 8 7 6 5 4 3 2 1

Printed in the United States of America.

Abstract

Leadership is a universal phenomenon that has preoccupied scholars, politicians, and others for centuries. It has been consistently identified as playing a critical role in the success or failure of organizations. Apart from organizational performance, researchers have consistently found a strong correlation between leadership styles and behaviors, and job satisfaction and performance of subordinates.

This book is intended to serve as a guide to basic principles of leadership. It begins with an overview of definitions and conceptions of leadership and continues with discussions of the roles and activities expected from an effective leader. Examples included are: personality traits and attributes which can be learned and perfected by persons that aspire to leadership positions and styles of leadership, which encompass the strategies used by leaders to engage with their followers and leadership in developing.

Keywords

Leadership; definitions of leadership; leadership roles; leadership activities; leadership personalities; leadership styles; leadership in developing countries

Contents

Preface

When formal interest in the study of leadership first began in the 19th and early 20th centuries, the so-called "great man" theory, which assumed that certain individual characteristics or traits could be found in leaders but not in nonleaders and that those characteristics could not be developed but must be inherited, was quite popular and many assumed that leaders were simply "born and not made." As time passed, however, the consensus within the community of leadership scholars and consultants shifted significantly to the current working proposition that although some people do indeed appear to be natural leaders from birth it is nonetheless possible for many others who have sufficient desire and willpower to develop into leaders by following a continuous process of work, self-study, education, training, and experience.[1]

Stogdill observed "there are almost as many different definitions of leadership as there are persons who have attempted to define the concept"[2] and there is no apparent limit to the creativity of researchers, management consultants, and actual practitioners in devising definitions

---

[1] Jago, A. 1982. "Leadership: Perspectives in Theory and Research." *Management Science* 28, no. 3, p. 315.Leadership remains one of the most popular topics among management books with recent entrants including Gordon, J. 2017. *Power of Positive Leadership*. New York, NY: Wiley; Craig, N. 2018. *Leading from Purpose: Clarity and Confidence to Act When It Matters*. London: Nicholas Brealey Publishing; Ashkenas, R., and B. Manville. 2018. *Harvard Business Review Leader's Handbook*. Cambridge MA: Harvard Business Press; Blanchard, K., and R. Broadwell. 2018. *Servant Leadership in Action: How You Can Achieve Great Relationships and Results*. Oakland, CA: Berrett-Koehler Publishers; Booher, D. 2017. *Communicate Like a Leader: Connecting Strategically to Coach, Inspire, and Get Things Done Paperback*. Oakland, CA: Berrett-Koehler Publishers; and George, B., et al. 2017. Authentic Leadership (HBR Emotional Intelligence Series).Cambridge MA: Harvard Business Press.

[2] Stogdill, R. 1974. *Handbook of Leadership: A Survey of Theory and Research*. New York, NY: The Free Press, p. 7.

and conceptions of leadership. Bass, one of the most well known of the modern scholars and pundits on leadership, argued that leadership was a "universal phenomenon" that could be defined and described as "an interaction between two or more members of a group that often involves a structuring or restructuring of the situation and the perception and expectations of the members."[3] A survey of other definitions and conceptualizations of leadership uncovers several common themes: the leader as a "person," including his or her traits and personality characteristics; the leader as an instrument of facilitating the needs and desires of the group of followers; leadership as an emerging effect of interaction; leadership as a process of influencing change in the conduct of people and motivating them to embrace and strive for specific goals; and leadership as a set of specific acts and behaviors that a person engages in while serving as a leader and attempting to direct and coordinate the work of his or her followers.

In practice, leadership is more than just personal traits and attributes or issuing directives from a list and, in fact, the reality is that leaders must be able to mix creative visioning with the often difficult and time-consuming tasks that must be completed to engage followers and enlist their support to move their organizations, and themselves, through turbulent changes. Practicing leadership begins by recognizing that four primary factors must be considered[4]:

1. The "leader," who must understand who he or she is and what he or she knows and realize that his or her success is dependent on the leader's ability to build trust and confidence among the followers and convince them to follow the leader's directives
2. The "followers," who all have their own needs and require different styles of leadership that can only be identified if a leader is attuned

---

[3] Bass, B. 1990. *Handbook of Leadership: Theory, Research and Managerial Applications*, 3rd ed. 19–20. New York, NY: The Free Press.

[4] U.S. Army. 1983. *Military Leadership: Field Manual*, 22–100. Washington, DC: U.S. Government Printing Office. (as cited in Clark, D. 2018. "Concepts of Leadership." *Big Dog and Little Dog's Performance Juxtaposition (blog)* http://nwlink.com/~donclark/leader/leadcon.html (accessed December 12, 2018).

to understanding human nature and the factors behind the needs, emotions, and motivations of the followers

3. The form and content of "communications" between the leader and his or her followers, which is interactive (i.e., two-way), frequently nonverbal and central to the development and maintenance of effective relationships

4. The "situation" or "context," which determines the actions that should be taken by the leader and the style that the leader should employ

Each of these factors is subject to a variety of forces that may impact the choices that a leader makes regarding his or her behaviors. For example, whereas the idea that a person must have certain inherited traits in order to be a leader has fallen into disrepute, the personality characteristics of the leader will invariably come into play as he or she assesses problems and opportunities and decides what steps need to be taken in working with followers. Other forces that will likely be relevant include the skills and experiences of the followers and how they interact with one another; the history, internal culture, and structure of the organization; the societal culture in which the organization operates; and competitive conditions, particularly the strategies being used by peer organizations to motivate their employees. Leaders must approach these factors, and the forces that influence them, with a solid analytical framework that can be referenced from time to time to ensure that they are paying attention to the things that really matter. A framework suggested by surveying the literature on leadership might include several elements discussed in more detail in this book: the requisite "skill set," which should be constructed and nurtured by reference to the appropriate performance imperatives for executive leadership; the roles and activities expected from an effective leader; personality traits and attributes which can be learned and perfected by persons aspiring to leadership positions; and styles of leadership, which encompass the strategies used by leaders to engage with their followers.

Emphasis on "performance imperatives" was stressed by Zaccaro and Klimoski, who counseled leaders about the importance of remembering the context of their actions as leaders and suggested that this could be accomplished by continuously assessing and developing the following categories of skills: cognitive, social, personal, political, technological, financial, and senior staffing.[5] Specific questions for leaders include the following:

- Does the leader have the requisite *cognitive* skills to effectively scan expansive and relatively unstructured external environments, process and make sense of the information collected from those scanning activities, and use that information to solve problems and forge long-term strategies?
- Does the leader have the *social* skills and competencies that are necessary and appropriate to forge and manage the relationships that are relevant to his or her position within the organizational hierarchy?
- Does the leader have the *personal* skills and attributes necessary for timely and skillful execution of activities such as career and reputation management and acquisition of authority and influence?
- Does the leader have the requisite *political* skills for acquisition of power, including powers of persuasion; and timely and judicious use of power, including the ability to handle and resolve conflicts and build coalitions?
- Does the leader have the skills necessary for coping with the dramatic and sweeping effects that *technological* advances have had on the way organizations operate and compete and the operational environment in which leaders must operate?
- Does the leader have the skills and tools necessary to successfully develop, implement, monitor, and adjust long- and short-term *financial* goals and objectives and strategies?
- Does the leader seek and hire candidates for positions at the *senior staffing* level in the organization, including other members of the executive team when the leader is the CEO,

---

[5] Zaccaro, S., and R. Klimoski. 2001. "The Nature of Organizational Leadership: An Introduction." In *The Nature of Organizational Leadership (Understanding the Performance Imperatives Confronting Today's Leaders)*, eds. S. Zaccaro and R. Klimoski, 1–41, 26–30. New York, NY: John Wiley & Sons.

who possess, or can easily and quickly acquire, the skills, dispositions, and capabilities required to respond appropriately to the demands associated with the earlier-described performance imperatives?

Although leaders can be distinguished from managers, leaders nonetheless are responsible for a number of the same functions typically categorized as "managerial" such as setting goals and designing strategic plans to achieve those goals, communicating directives to other members of the organization, overseeing execution of the organizational strategy, and setting guidelines for motivating organizational members and assessing their performance. The specific roles and activities of a particular leader will vary depending on where he or she is located within the organizational hierarchy and will also be influenced by other factors such as the type of business engaged in by the organization, the environmental conditions that the organization is facing, the stage of the organization's development, and the leader's role in the launch of the organization (e.g., a "founder").[6] However, all leaders, regardless of their position or other circumstances, should be prepared to engage in certain core roles and activities including selecting and defining goals and objectives for the organization and designing strategic plans to achieve those goals and objectives; communicating ideas about their vision for the organization and providing directions to other members of the organization regarding actions to be taken to realize the vision; designing and implementing an effective organizational structure that promotes efficient flow of information and collaboration among members of the organization; implementing human resources management practices that support their vision and provide members of the organization with access to training necessary to maintain and improve the skills required for them to positively participate in the execution of the vision; and engaging in behaviors that support organizational members and enhance their feelings of personal worth and importance.

---

[6] Muczyk, J., and T. Adler. 2002. "An Attempt at a Consentience Regarding Formal Leadership." *Journal of Leadership and Organizational Studies* 9, no. 2, pp. 2–17.

There is no doubt that extensive resources have been devoted to the search for traits and attributes of effective leaders and, as mentioned earlier, a person seeking to become a leader need not despair if it all does not seem to come naturally. The question, or course, is identifying the specific personality traits and attributes that are most closely aligned with effective leadership. Answers provided by researchers include emotional self-awareness; self-control; credibility; trustworthiness and integrity; adaptability; achievement orientation and ambition; a strong desire to influence and lead others and willingness to assume responsibility; the ability to use power intelligently to achieve desire goals; social awareness and empathy; social skills and ability to build relationships and promote cooperation; relevant cognitive ability (i.e., strong analytical ability, good judgment, and the capacity to think strategically and multidimensionally); and a high degree of task-related knowledge about the organization, industry, and technical matters.

The form and content of communications between the leader and the followers, and among the followers themselves, are heavily dependent on the leader's chosen "leadership style," which has been defined as "the manner and approach of providing direction, motivating people and achieving objectives."[7] Although there a number of different models of leadership style, three fundamental dimensions are often represented: the leader's approach to influencing the behavior of his or her followers; the manner in which decisions regarding the direction of the group are made, with a specific emphasis on the level of participation offered to followers; and the balance struck between goal attainment and maintaining harmony within the group (sometimes referred to as group "maintenance").[8] For example, two alternative approaches to influencing the behavior of followers are the transactional leadership, which views the leader–follower relationship as a process of exchange, and transformational leadership, which relies on the leader's ability to communicate a clear and acceptable vision and related goals that engender intense emotion among followers

---

[7] Fertman, C., and J. van Liden. October 1999. "Character Education: An Essential Ingredient for Youth Leadership Development." *NASSP Bulletin* 83, no. 609, pp. 9–15.

[8] Scholl, R. 2000. *Changing Leadership Style.*

that motivates them to buy into and pursue the leader's vision. Contrasting styles for decision-making are found when distinguishing authoritarian (autocratic) and participative (democratic) leaders. The balance between goals and maintenance is emphasized in those models that analyze the degree to which the leader exhibits task and/or relationship orientations in his or her interactions with followers (e.g., "Country Club Leadership," with a high concern for people and low concern for production, versus "Produce or Perish Leadership," with a low concern for people and high concern for production). Other important theories and models of leadership styles include emotional intelligence and leadership styles, servant leadership, Silicon Valley leadership, and sustainable leadership. Although leadership styles are often introduced as static and fixed, the reality is that appropriate leadership styles do tend to change as time goes by and the leader must be able and willing to attempt to change his or her style or step aside in favor of someone else who is better prepared to provide the right style for the particular situation.

It is important to understand that the field of leadership studies has long been primarily focused on western leadership styles and practices.[9] This occurred for various reasons including the location of the critical mass of researchers in the United States and the fact that most companies operated primarily in the United States with some cautious expansion into foreign markets with similar linguistic and cultural traditions. However, several factors—globalization of the workforce, expansion of operations into numerous countries and regions around the world, and exposure to increase global competition—has forced leadership scholars to incorporate culture into their research and theories because leaders of businesses of all sizes in all countries must be prepared to interact with customers and other business partners from different cultures and leaders of larger companies have the additional challenge of managing multinational organizations and aligning a global corporate culture with multiple

---

[9] For a general introduction to the area of leadership studies including definitional concepts and a history of the evolution of leadership studies, see "History and Evolution of Leadership Studies" In "Leadership: A Library of Resources for Sustainable Entrepreneurs" prepared and distributed by the Sustainable Entrepreneurship Project (www.seproject.org).

and diverging national cultures. There has also been a growing recognition that the study of leadership in developing countries, and training of prospective leaders in those countries, is important because leaders in developing countries can play a pivotal role in resolving multiple collection action problems that impede social development and economic growth in those countries.[10]

---

[10] de Ver, H.L. April 2008. "Leadership, Politics and Development: A Literature Survey (Development Leadership Program, Background Paper)." www.dlprog. org/ftp/.../Leadership,%20Politics%20and%20Development.pdf, 4

CHAPTER 1

Definitions and Conceptions
of Leadership

Introduction

Leadership is a universal phenomenon that has preoccupied scholars, politicians, and others for centuries.[1] Zagoršek observed:

> the simultaneous appearance of social institutions such as government, organized religion, and a significant role for individual leaders argues that there may well be something about people in complex organizations that provides a social value in having "leaders"—they arise to fulfill a basic social function.[2]

In the management context, leadership has been consistently identified as playing a critical role in the success or failure of organizations and some surveys have pegged up to 45 percent of an organization's performance on the quality and effectiveness of its leadership team.[3] Apart from organizational performance, researchers have consistently found a strong

---

[1] See, e.g., Bass, B.M. 1997. "Does the Transactional-Transformational Leadership Paradigm Transcend Organizational and National Boundaries?" *American Psychologist* 52, no. 2, pp. 130–39; and Peterson, M., and J. Hunt. 1997. "International Perspectives on International Leadership." *Leadership Quarterly* 8, no. 3, pp. 203–32.

[2] Zagoršek, H. 2004. *Assessing the Impact of National Culture on Leadership: A Six Nation Study*. Ljubljana.

[3] Bass, B.M. 1990. *Bass & Stogdill's Handbook of Leadership: Theory, Research, and Managerial Applications*, 3rd ed. New York, NY: Free Press; Day, D., and R. Lord. 1988. "Executive Leadership and Organizational Performance: Suggestions for a New Theory and Methodology." *Journal of Management* 14, no. 3, pp. 453–64.

correlation between leadership styles and behaviors and the job satisfaction and performance of subordinates.[4]

During the early years of serious research in the leadership area the focus was primarily on western leadership styles and practices. This occurred for various reasons including the location of the critical mass of researchers in the United States and the fact that most companies operated primarily in the United States with some cautious expansion into foreign markets with similar linguistic and cultural traditions. However, several factors—globalization of the workforce, expansion of operations into numerous countries and regions around the world, and exposure to increase global competition—have forced leadership scholars to incorporate culture into their research and theories because leaders of businesses of all sizes in all countries must be prepared to interact with customers and other business partners from different cultures and leaders of larger companies have the additional challenge of managing multinational organizations and aligning a global corporate culture with multiple and diverging national cultures.[5] Another driving force in the push for more

---

[4] Schriesheim, C., and L. Neider. 1996. "Path-Goal Theory: The Long and Winding Road." *Leadership Quarterly* 7, pp. 317–21; Howell, J., and D. Costley. 2001. *Understanding Behaviors for Effective Leadership*. Upper Saddle River, NJ: Prentice Hall.

[5] Zagoršek, H. 2004. *Assessing the Impact of National Culture on Leadership: A Six Nation Study*. Ljubljana. With regard to managing the cultural aspects of multinational corporations, see Miroshnik, V. 2002. "Culture and International Management: A Review." *Journal of Management Development* 21, no. 7, pp. 521–44. Excellent reviews of the literature relating to international and cross-cultural leadership research can be found in House, R.J., N.S. Wright, and R.N. Aditya. 1997. "Cross-Cultural Research on Organizational Leadership: A Critical Analysis and a Proposed Theory." In *New Perspectives on International Industrial/Organizational Psychology*, eds. P. Earle and M. Erez, 535–625. San Francisco; Dorfman, P. 1996. "International and Cross-Cultural Leadership Research." In *Handbook for International Management Research*, eds. B. Punnett and O. Shenkar, 267–349. Oxford, UK: Blackwell; Dorfman, P.W. 1996. "International and Cross-cultural Leadership Research." In *Handbook for International Management Research*, eds. B. Punnett and O. Shenkar, 2nd ed. Ann Arbor, MI: University of Michigan; Dickson, M.W., D.N. Den Hartog, and J.K. Mitchelson. 2003. "Research on Leadership in a Cross-Cultural Context: Making Progress, and

work on the relationship between culture and leadership has been the emergence of an international research community that includes scholars living, working, and observing in all parts of the world and this has led to the expansion of the scope of inquiry to include such diverse topics as leadership styles of managers and entrepreneurs in Russia and other countries that were formerly part of the Soviet Union.[6]

Definitions of Leadership

The effective study and understanding of leadership begins with constructing a workable definition of the term "leadership." Interestingly, although leadership has been rigorously studied and discussed for centuries, a consensus regarding how the term "leadership" can and should be defined has been elusive. In this regard, Stogdill observed that "there are almost as many definitions of leadership as there are persons who have attempted to define the concept" and Fiedler wrote that "[t]here are almost as many definitions of leadership as there are leadership theories— and there are almost as many theories of leadership as there are psychologists working in the field."[7] Dickson et al. succinctly described leadership

---

Raising New Questions." *The Leadership Quarterly* 14, no. 6, pp. 729–68. and Scandura, T., and P. Dorfman. April 2004. "Leadership Research in an International and Cross-cultural Context." *The Leadership Quarterly* 15, no. 2, pp. 277–307. For further discussion of the study of cross-cultural leadership in the context of the general evolution of cross-cultural studies, see "Cross-Cultural Leadership Studies" prepared and distributed by the Sustainable Entrepreneurship Project (www.seproject.org).

[6] See, e.g., Ardichvili, A., R. Cardozo, and A. Gasparishvili. 1998. "Leadership Styles and Management Practices of Russian Entrepreneurs: Implications for Transferability of Westerns HRD Interventions." *Human Resource Development Quarterly* 9, no. 2, pp. 145–55; and Ardichvili, A., and K. Kuchinke. 2002. "Leadership Styles and Cultural Values Among Managers and Subordinates: A Comparative Study of Four Countries of the Former Soviet Union, Germany and the US." *Human Resource Development International* 5, no. 1, pp. 99–117.

[7] Stogdill, R. 1974. *Handbook of Leadership*, 259. New York, NY: Free Press; Fiedler, F. 1971. "Validation and Extension of the Contingency Model of Leadership Effectiveness: A Review of Empirical Findings." *Psychological Bulletin* 76, no. 2, p. 128.

as involving "disproportionate influence" and noted that leadership roles around the world are universally associated with power and status and that it is therefore important to understand how power and status are distributed in a society in order to obtain a clear picture of leadership roles in that society.[8] The researchers involved in the Global Leadership and Organizational Effectiveness (GLOBE) project defined leadership as "… the ability of an individual to influence, motivate, and enable others to contribute toward the effectiveness and success of the organizations of which they are members."[9] The potential influence of leaders is substantial as the following observation of the GLOBE researchers illustrates:

> When individuals think about effective leader behaviors, they are more influenced by the value they place on the desired future than their perception of current realities. Our results, therefore, suggest that leaders are seen as the society's instruments for change. They are seen as the embodiment of the ideal state of affairs.[10]

Eckmann offered a short and not inclusive list of leadership definitions from a variety of sources and activities that included the following[11]:

- The creative and directive force of morale
- A process of mutual stimulation which, by the successful interplay of relevant individual differences, controls human energy in the pursuit of a common cause
- The process by which an agent induces a subordinate to behave in a desired manner

---

[8] Dickson, M.W., D.N. Den Hartog, and J.K. Mitchelson. 2003. "Research on Leadership in a Cross-cultural Context: Making Progress, and Raising New Questions." *The Leadership Quarterly* 14, no. 6, pp. 729–68, p. 737.

[9] House, R.J., P.J. Hanges, M. Javidan, P.W. Dorfman, and V. Gupta, eds. 2004. *Culture, Leadership, and Organizations: The GLOBE Study of 62 Societies*, 15. Thousand Oaks CA: Sage.

[10] Id. at pp. 275–76.

[11] See Eckmann, H. 2018. "History of Leadership Studies." http://jameslconsulting.com/documents/history-of-leadership-studies.pdf (accessed December 10, 2018) (includes citations to sources of leadership definitions)

- Directing and coordinating the work of group member, a definition that is more appropriate for management activities
- An interpersonal relation in which others comply between they want to, not because they have to, a formulation similar to the concept of "transformational" leadership discussed elsewhere in this guide.
- The process of influencing an organized group toward accomplishing its goals and the creation of conditions for the team to be effective, both closely linked to the study and practice of team leadership
- The thing that wins battles, a contribution by General Patton

Muczyk and Holt defined "leadership," in a general sense, as

the process whereby one individual influences other group members toward the attainment of defined group or organizational goals. In other words, the leadership role describes the relationship between the manager and his or her subordinates that results in the satisfactory execution of subordinates' assignments and, thereby, the attainment of the important goals for which the leader is responsible and is instrumental in setting. At the very minimum, leadership requires providing direction and impetus for subordinates to act in the desired direction.[12]

They believed that it was important to distinguish leadership per se from actions or behaviors of leaders that are actually "enablers" or "facilitators" of effective leadership, such as the traits, tendencies, and practices of leaders with respect to such things as planning, communicating, motivating, and decision-making.

---

[12] Muczyk, J., and D. Holt. May 2008. "Toward a Cultural Contingency Model of Leadership." *Journal of Leadership & Organizational Studies* 14, no. 4, pp. 277–86, 280. (citing also Muczyk, J., and T. Adler. 2002. "An Attempt at a Consentience Regarding Formal Leadership." *Journal of Leadership and Organizational Studies* 9, no. 2, pp. 2–17; and Yuki, G. 1998. *Leadership in Organisations*. Upper Saddle River, NJ: Prentice Hall.)

Muczyk and Holt noted that the GLOBE researchers claimed to have found evidence of the following "universal attributes that facilitate leadership effectiveness": integrity (being trustworthy, just, and honest); charismatic–visionary (having foresight and planning ahead); charismatic–inspirational (being positive, dynamic, encouraging, and motivating and building confidence); and team builder (being communicative, informed, a coordinator, and a team integrator).[13] In turn, "universal attributes that impede effectiveness" according to the GLOBE researchers included self-protection (being a loner and asocial); malevolence (being non-cooperative and irritable), and autocratic behavior (being dictatorial). The effectiveness of other attributes, such as individualism, status consciousness, and risk taking, were found to vary based on the cultural context (i.e., culturally contingent) in the GLOBE survey. Muczyk and Holt conceded that the leadership "attributes" identified by the GLOBE researchers were important to the extent that they could be analyzed as facilitators or inhibitors of effective leadership; however, they cautioned that those attributes should not be confused with leadership itself. In their view, for example, having integrity, being visionary and/or inspirational, or being adept at team building was not "leadership," but those traits could be presumed to be extremely useful tools in successfully filling the role of a leader, namely influencing followers toward attainment of group goals. Similarly, "communication skills, motivational techniques, and influence strategies are the means to leadership success, and not leadership itself."[14]

---

[13] Muczyk, J., and D. Holt. May 2008. "Toward a Cultural Contingency Model of Leadership." *Journal of Leadership & Organizational Studies* 14, no. 4, pp. 277–86, 280. (adapted from Javidan, M., P. Dorfman, M. de Luque, and R. House. February 2006. "In the Eye of the Beholder: Cross Cultural Lessons in Leadership from Project GLOBE." *Academy of Management Perspectives* 20, no. 1, pp. 67–90.) For detailed discussion of the work of the GLOBE researchers, see "Cross-Cultural Leadership Studies" prepared and distributed by the Sustainable Entrepreneurship Project.

[14] Muczyk, J., and T. Adler. 2002. "An Attempt at a Consentience Regarding Formal Leadership." *Journal of Leadership and Organizational Studies* 9, no. 2, pp. 2–17 (citing Yukl, G., and C. Falbe. 1990. "Influence Tactics in Upward, Downward, and Lateral Influence Attempts." *Journal of Applied Psychology* 75, no. 2, pp. 132–40.)

Although there appears to be a clear consensus that leadership is an important topic within the fields of business and organizational studies, one of the most significant challenges for researchers, and the principal basis for the entire field of cross-cultural leadership studies, is the anecdotal evidence that points to the realization that leadership has a very different meaning depending upon the cultural context. For example, the researchers in the GLOBE study collected and presented the following statements taken from interviews with managers from various countries to support the proposition that leadership is "culturally contingent" because various societies (i.e., Americans, Arabs, Asians, English, Eastern Europeans, French, Germans, Latin Americans, and Russians) tended to glorify the concept of leadership and considered it reasonable to discuss leadership in the context of both the political and the organizational arenas whereas people who came from other societies, such as the Netherlands and the Scandinavian countries, often had distinctly different views of leadership[15]:

- "Americans appreciate two kinds of leaders. They seek empowerment from leaders who grant autonomy and delegate authority to subordinates. They also respect the bold, forceful, confident, and risk-taking leader, as personified by John Wayne."
- "The Dutch place emphasis on egalitarianism and are skeptical about the value of leadership. Terms like leader and manager carry a stigma. If a father is employed as a manager, Dutch children will not admit it to their schoolmates."
- "Arabs worship their leaders—*as long as they are in power!*"
- "Iranians seek power and strength in their leaders."
- "Malaysians expect their leaders to behave in a manner that is humble, modest, and dignified."
- "The French appreciate two kinds of leaders. De Gaulle and Mitterand are examples. De Gaulle is an example of a strong charismatic leader. Mitterand is an example of a consensus builder, coalition former and effective negotiator."

---

[15] House, R.J., and N. Mansor. 1999. "Cultural Influences on Leadership and Organizations." *Advances in Global Leadership*, Vol. 1, 171–233. Greenwich, CT: JAI Press, Inc.

The diversity of opinion among managers from around the world elicited in an informal setting was sufficient encouragement for the GLOBE researchers to embark upon the rigorous multicultural study of perceptions of leadership that is described in detail elsewhere in this publication.

Chronology of Leadership Definitions

An interesting approach to definitions of leadership is a compilation based on the work of Rost that traces how definitional concepts changed as leadership studies evolved from 1900 through the first decade of the 21stcentury[16]:

Definitions from 1900 to 1929 emphasized control, centralization of power, and domination of subordinates by their leader. One definition that summed all this up viewed leadership as "the ability to impress the will of the leader on those led and induce obedience, respect, loyalty, and cooperation."[17]

During the 1930s, leadership transitioned from "dominance" to "influence" as researchers became interested in studying the interaction of specific personality traits (i.e., the trait school of leadership discussed elsewhere in this guide) of the leader with followers in his or her group. Leaders were thought to use their personality characteristics to change, or influence, the activities, attitudes, and values of their followers and, in turn, the leader was also influenced by his or her followers as they interacted together in the group situation.

The emphasis on leadership dynamics with groups continued during the 1940s and leaders were expected to influence, persuade, and direct the members of their group without excessive reliance on the power and authority of their position. A common definition of leadership during

---

[16] See Northouse, P. 2016. "The History of Leadership Studies and Evolution of Leadership Theories." June 14, 2016. https://toughnickel.com/business/The-History-of-Leadership-Studies-and-Evolution-of-Leadership-Theories (accessed December 10, 2018). See also Rost, J.C. 1991. *Leadership for the Twenty-First Century*. Westport, CT: Praeger Publishers.

[17] Rost, J.C. 1991. *Leadership for the Twenty-First Century*, 47. Westport, CT: Praeger Publishers.(citing Moore, B.V. 1927. "The May Conference on Leadership." *Personnel Journal* 6, no. 124, pp. 124–28).

this period was that it was "the behavior of an individual while he is involved in directing group activities."[18]

In the 1950s, one school of leadership viewed it simply as "what leaders do in groups"[19] and saw leaders as being in a noncoercive relationship with their followers and responsible for facilitating the group's efforts to develop and pursue shared goals. Others, however, focused on domination in the leader–follower relationship and viewed leadership as "the art of getting what one … wants and making people like it."[20]

In the 1960s, the dominant theme was the role of leaders in influencing followers to achieve shared goals. Influence came from adroitly engaging in "a rational exchange of values in which followers barter their supports for political decisions to their liking."[21]

Leadership in the 1970s was seen as the process of "initiating and maintaining groups or organizations to accomplish group or organizational goals."[22] Rost mentioned the introduction and development of the "leader–member exchange theory of leadership" during this period and the need for leaders to be adept at communication and persuasion and avoid resisting "counter-influence" by their followers and relying on tools of power to impose their will.[23] The path-goal theory, which was based on Vroom's expectancy theory, was developed in the early 1970s and was based on the assumption that subordinates would be motivated if they

---

[18] Id. at pp. 49-50 (citing Hemphill, J. 1949. "The Leader and his Group." *Journal of Educational Research* 28, pp. 225–29, 245–46.)

[19] Id. at p. 50 citing Gibb, C.A. 1954. "Leadership." In *Handbook of Social Psychology*, ed. G. Lindzey, 877–920, 2 vols. Reading, MA: Addison-Wesley.

[20] Id. at p. 52 citing Titus, C. 1950. *The Processes of Leadership.* Dubuque, IA: Brown.

[21] Schlesinger, J. 1967. "Political Careers and Political Leadership" In *Political Leadership in Industrialized Societies*, ed. L. Edinger, 266–93, 266. New York, NY: Wiley.

[22] Rost, J.C. 1991. *Leadership for the Twenty-First Century*, 59. Westport, CT: Praeger Publishers.

[23] For more on the "exchange theory of leadership," see Jacobs, T. 1970. *Leadership and Exchange Informal Organizations.* Alexandria, VA: Human Resources Research Organization; and Hollander, E.P. 1978. *Leadership Dynamics.* New York, NY: The Free Press.

thought they were capable of the work (or high level of self-efficacy), believed their efforts would result in a certain outcome or reward, and believed the outcome or reward would be worthwhile.[24]

The leadership definitions used during the 1980s reflected the various schools of leadership that had developed up to and during that period. Influence remained an important concept and leadership was often described as the process of influencing, inspiring, and persuading followers to achieve organizational objectives. However, consistent with developments in earlier decades, leadership was not something that simply came down from the mountain where the leader sat but instead arose in the context of an "influence relationship among leaders and followers who intend real changes that reflect their mutual purposes." In other words, effective leaders are able to mobilize their followers to realize goals mutually held by both leaders and followers.[25] Some definitions of leadership emphasized that leaders were persons who possessed or developed specific traits. The 1980s also saw the emergence of the concept of the "transformational" leader who was able to transform his or her followers to higher levels of motivation and/or morality. Transformational leadership, which was first described by James McGregor Burns and then expounded upon by Bernard Bass, has remained one of the most widely researched types of leadership well into the 2010s.[26]

The 1990s saw the popularization of servant leadership, an idea that had its roots in the essays that Greenleaf published in the 1970s that

---

[24] See Northouse, P. 2016. "The History of Leadership Studies and Evolution of Leadership Theories." June 14, 2016. https://toughnickel.com/business/The-History-of-Leadership-Studies-and-Evolution-of-Leadership-Theories (accessed December 10, 2018).

[25] MacGregor Burns, J. 1979. *Leadership*. New York, NY: Harper Torchbooks. ("Leadership over human beings is exercised when persons with certain motives and purposes mobilize, in competition or conflict with others, institutional, political, psychological, and other resources so as to arouse, engage, and satisfy the motives of followers")

[26] See Northouse, P. 2016. "The History of Leadership Studies and Evolution of Leadership Theories." June 14, 2016, https://toughnickel.com/business/The-History-of-Leadership-Studies-and-Evolution-of-Leadership-Theories (accessed December 10, 2018).

proposed a new type of leadership focused on the follower. The 1990s and 2000s also saw increased interest in authentic leadership, first suggested by George, with the development of the Authentic Leadership Questionnaire and a focus on various aspects of authentic leadership including self-awareness, relational transparency, balanced processing, and internalized moral perspective.[27] Other concepts of leadership that gained some degree of prominence during the period discussed earlier included implicit leadership theory based on the proposition that individuals have implicit beliefs, convictions, and assumptions concerning attributes and behaviors that help that individual distinguish between leaders and followers, effective leaders from ineffective leaders, and moral leaders from evil leaders; and situational leadership theory, proposed by Hersey and Blanchard, that is based on the concept that leaders choose the leadership style (i.e., directing, coaching, supporting, or delegating) based on the maturity or developmental level of the follower.[28]

Zaccaro and Klimoski's Defining Elements of Organizational Leadership

Rather than offer up another definition of leadership, Zaccaro and Klimoski elected to collect and describe what they considered to be the "central defining elements of organizational leadership" based on their review and assessment of the ideas that have come forth from the community of leadership scholars.[29] Specifically, they argued that

---

[27] For more information on "authentic leadership," see George, B., et al. 2017. Authentic Leadership. HBR Emotional Intelligence Series Cambridge MA: Harvard Business Press.

[28] See Northouse, P. 2016. "The History of Leadership Studies and Evolution of Leadership Theories." June 14, 2016, https://toughnickel.com/business/The-History-of-Leadership-Studies-and-Evolution-of-Leadership-Theories (accessed December 10, 2018).

[29] Zaccaro, S., and R. Klimoski. 2001. "The Nature of Organizational Leadership: An Introduction." In The Nature of Organizational Leadership (Understanding the Performance Imperatives Confronting Today's Leaders), eds. S. Zaccaro and R. Klimoski, 1–41, 6. New York, NY: John Wiley & Sons.

Organizational leadership involves processes and proximal outcomes (e.g., worker commitment) that contribute to the development and achievement of the organizational purpose.

Organizational leadership is identified by the application of nonroutine influence on organizational life.

Leader influence is grounded in cognitive, social, and political processes.

Organizational leadership is inherently bounded by system characteristics and dynamics. In other words, leadership is contextually defined and caused.[30]

Leadership and Organizational Purpose

Zaccaro and Klimoski noted that "organizational purpose is operationalized as a direction for collective action" and that leadership positions within the organization are created as a means for helping the subunits of the organization to achieve the purposes for which they were created within the larger organizational system.[31] The role, or function, of an organizational leader is to engage in processes directed at defining, establishing, identifying or translating the organizational purpose for his or her followers, and facilitating or enabling the organizational processes that should, if done well, result in the achievement of that purpose. In order to be effective in this role, the leader must be continuously involved in the development and attainment of organizational mission, vision, strategy, goals and plans, and the design of the tasks associated with implementation of the plans. Zaccaro and Klimoski believed that responsibility for organizational purpose and direction lay with senior organizational leaders and that those leaders must have the cognitive resources necessary to build the frame of reference necessary to forge organizational strategy. They also noted that organizational strategy reflected, in part, the personal and career objectives of the senior leader, an interesting observation

---

[30] Id. The discussion in the following sections is adapted from the cited work of Zaccaro and Klimoski at pp. 6–13.

[31] Id.

that was integrated into their theory about the performance imperative of organizational leaders described elsewhere in this publication.

Leadership as Nonroutine Influence

Zaccaro and Klimoski argued that "leadership does not reside in the routine activities of organizational work" but rather "occurs in response to, or in anticipation of, non-routine organizational events."[32] They based their arguments on the observations of Katz and Kahn, who wrote that "the essence of organizational leadership [is] the influential increment over and above mechanical compliance with the routine directives of the organization."[33] Zaccaro and Klimoski defined "non-routine events" as "any situation that constitutes a potential or actual hindrance to organizational goal progress" and suggested that leaders must be prepared and equipped to be continuously involved in constructing the nature of organizational problems; developing and evaluating potential solutions to those problems; and planning, implementing, and monitoring the chosen solutions in complex social domains. Zaccaro and Klimoski noted that the emphasis on the "non-routine" influence of the leader reflected several other important points: Leaders must respond to "ill-defined" problems with unspecified starting parameters and permissible solution paths and solution goals; the leadership process is only relevant in situation where there is decision discretion, thus creating an opportunity for leadership; and leadership intervention is not needed with respect to "team or organizational actions that are completely specified by procedure or practice."[34] Zaccaro and Klimoski referred to the leader's responsibilities and challenges with respect to nonroutine events as a "functional or social problem-solving perspective of leadership" and noted that leaders

---

[32] Id. at p. 8.

[33] Katz, D., and R. Kahn. 1978. *The Social Psychology of Organizations*, 528, 2nd ed. New York, NY: Wiley 528.

[34] Zaccaro, S., and R. Klimoski. 2001. "The Nature of Organizational Leadership: An Introduction." In *The Nature of Organizational Leadership* (Understanding the Performance Imperatives Confronting Today's Leaders), eds. S. Zaccaro and R. Klimoski, 1–41, 8–9. New York, NY: John Wiley & Sons.

must operate within a contextual framework that presents fundamental performance imperatives that demand that leaders make decisions regarding which problems are important and which solutions are appropriate. These performance imperatives (e.g., technological, financial, senior staffing, etc.) are explained elsewhere in this guide.

Leadership as Managing Social and Cognitive Phenomena

Zaccaro and Klimoski correctly observed that social or interpersonal influence processes (i.e., "persuasion") are an important element in many definitions of leadership. They did not quarrel with the notion that leadership required management of social phenomena; however, they argued that "execution of effective cognitive processes is equally critical to leader effectiveness."[35] For example, Zaccaro and Klimoski argued that the cognitive requirements of the leadership position could be seen in the responsibility of leaders to interpret and model environmental events for members of the organization, determine the nature of the organization problems that need to be solved, engage in long-term strategic thinking, and plan collective action. They cited the following quote from the work of Jacobs and Jaques to support their argument:

> Executive leaders "add value" to their organizations in large part by giving a sense of understanding and purpose to the overall activities of the organization. In excellent organizations, there almost always is a feeling that the "boss" knows what he is doing, that he has shared this information downward, that it makes sense, and that it is going to work.[36]

Importantly, Zaccaro and Klimoski commented that all organizational leaders, not just those at the top of the hierarchy (i.e., the senior

---

[35] Id. at p. 10.

[36] Jacobs, T., and E. Jaques. 1991. "Executive Leadership." In *Handbook of Military Psychology*, eds. R. Gal and A. Manglesdorff, 434. New York, NY: Wiley.

leaders), need to interpret their operating environment and communicate their understanding of that environment to their own constituencies.

Leadership and Organizational Context

Perhaps the strongest criticism that Zaccaro and Klimoski made with respect to many of the recognized theories of organizational leadership was that they were "context free" and thus failed to adequately take into account structural considerations that they believed significantly affected and moderated the conduct and effectiveness of organizational leaders. Zaccaro and Klimoski argued that a useful and realistic model of organizational leadership had to explicitly incorporate organizational context.[37] They were particularly interested in ensuring that the influence of the organizational level at which the leadership occurs was taken into account. Citing the prior research work of Zaccaro himself, as well as Jacobs and Jaques and Katz and Kahn,[38] Zaccaro and Klimoski maintained that the fundamental demands and work requirements of leaders change at different levels and that the "hierarchical context" of leadership "has profound effects on the personal, interpersonal, and organizational choices that can be made, as well as the import that a given choice might have."[39] They described the three distinct patterns of organizational leadership specified by Katz and Kahn, which are described elsewhere in this publication, and

---

[37] Zaccaro, S., and R. Klimoski. 2001. "The Nature of Organizational Leadership: An Introduction." In *The Nature of Organizational Leadership* (Understanding the Performance Imperatives Confronting Today's Leaders), eds. S. Zaccaro and R. Klimoski, 1–41, 12. New York, NY: John Wiley & Sons.

[38] See Zaccaro, S. 1996. *Models and Theories of Executive Leadership: A Conceptual/Empirical Review and Integration.* Alexandria, VA: U.S. Army Research Institute for the Behavioral and Social Sciences; Jacobs, T., and E. Jaques. 1987. "Leadership in Complex Systems." In *Human Productivity Enhancement*, ed. J. Zeidner. New York, NY: Praeger; and Katz, D., and R.L. Kahn. 1978. *The Social Psychology of Organizations*, 2nd ed. New York, NY: Wiley.

[39] Zaccaro, S., and R. Klimoski. 2001. "The Nature of Organizational Leadership: An Introduction." In *The Nature of Organizational Leadership* (Understanding the Performance Imperatives Confronting Today's Leaders), eds. S. Zaccaro and R. Klimoski, 1–41, 12. New York, NY: John Wiley & Sons.

suggested that the distribution of these patterns across organizational levels provided support for the presence of significant qualitative differences between the nature of junior and senior leadership, an idea explored in more detail in the discussion of "levels of leadership" as follows.

Barnard Bass

Bass, one of the most well known of the modern scholars and pundits on leadership, argued that leadership was a "universal phenomenon" that could be defined and described as "an interaction between two or more members of a group that often involves a structuring or restructuring of the situation and the perception and expectations of the members."[40] Bass is perhaps most famous for his championing of "transformational leadership" and thus it is not surprising for him to have declared that "[l]eaders are agents of change—persons whose acts affect other people more than other people's acts affect them" and that "[l]eadership occurs when one group member modifies the motivation or competencies of others in the group."[41]

In addition to providing his own definition and conceptualization of leadership, Bass compiled the ideas and efforts of other scholars on the question into various groupings. One grouping includes conceptions that are based on the assumption that leaders work to understand and satisfy the needs of followers and that goals, roles, and responsibilities within the group emerge from interactions between the leader and his or her followers:

"The leader as the focus of group processes": One scholar argued that "the leader is always the nucleus of a tendency"[42] and Bass observed that this conception assumed that leaders were initially influenced by the needs of their followers and that once a leader understood the collective will of his or her followers the leader's role was to focus the energies of the followers in the appropriate direction.[43]

---

[40] Bass, B.M. 1990. *Handbook of Leadership: Theory, Research and Managerial Applications*, 19–20, 3rd ed. New York, NY: The Free Press.

[41] Id.

[42] Cooley, C. 1902. *Human Nature and the Social Order*. New York: Scribners.

[43] Bass, B.M. 1990. *Handbook of Leadership: Theory, Research and Managerial Applications*, 3rd ed. New York, NY: The Free Press.

"Leadership as an instrument of goal achievement": Similar to the earlier-described emphasis on understanding and executing the collective will of his or her followers, this conception focuses on a leader's ability to satisfy the needs of the group and achieve the goals set for the group. According to Bass, the key roles of the leader include motivating and coordinating the group in the accomplishment of its goals, transforming followers, creating visions of the goals that may be attained, and, finally, articulating for followers the actions to be taken in order to achieve those goals.[44]

"Leadership as an emerging effect of interaction": Extending the influence of the collective will of the group in the prior conceptions of leadership, proponents of this conception argue that the group not only dictates the goals to be pursued but also selects the leaders and assigns them their status and responsibilities. Bass emphasized the process of interaction associated with this conception of leadership and commented that "leadership truly only exists when it is acknowledged and conferred by other members of the group."[45]

Another grouping, described as "leadership as personality and its effects," was developed by personality theorists who "equated leadership with strength of personality" and saw leaders as being those members of a group who possessed the "greatest number of desirable traits of personality and character."[46] According to Bass, personality theorists saw

---

[44] Id. at pp. 15–16; and Davis, R. 1942. *The Fundamentals of Top Management*. New York, NY: Harper.

[45] Bass, B.M. 1990. *Handbook of Leadership: Theory, Research and Managerial Applications*, 16, 3rd ed. New York, NY: The Free Press. See also Stogdill, R., and C. Shartle. 1948. "Methods for Determining Patterns of Leadership Behavior in Relation to Organization Structure and Objectives." *Journal of Applied Psychology* 32, no. 3, p. 286, 287. ("Leadership is a process of interaction between persons who are participating in goal oriented group activities").

[46] Bass, B.M. 1990. *Handbook of Leadership: Theory, Research and Managerial Applications*, 12, 3rd ed. New York, NY: The Free Press; Bowden, A. 1926. "A Study of the Personality of Student Leaders in the United States." *Journal of Abnormal and Social Psychology* 21, pp. 149–60; Bingham, W. 1927. "Leadership." In *The Psychological Foundations of Management*, ed. H.C. Metcalfe. New York, NY: Shaw.

leadership as a "one-way effect"—followers had no influence on their leaders—and believed that leaders possessed qualities that distinguished them from their followers.[47] This grouping would include the so-called "great man" theories that assume that leadership is an inherent capability that is only within the reach of a chosen few who are "born to lead" and trait theories that argue that people are only qualified for leadership if they possess certain inherited traits or personality characteristics.

A third grouping paints leadership as an exercise is power and authoritarianism. One conception, referred to as "leadership as the art of inducing compliance," implies that effective leadership is "the ability to handle men so as to achieve the most with the least friction and the greatest cooperation" and "the ability to impress the will of the leader on those led and induce obedience, respect, loyalty, and cooperation."[48] According to Bass, the leader's job under this conception was to exert his or her influence so as to mold the group and its actions to the leader's will.[49] A related conception constructs leadership as a "power relation" and represents the potentially extreme and undesirable consequences of a leader's efforts to induce compliance to his or her will and recognizes that leaders have often transformed leadership opportunities into an "overt power relation" amounting to an authoritarian leadership style that is now generally rejected as ineffective by most leadership theorists.[50]

A fourth grouping includes conceptions that became popular as a response to heavy-handed authoritarian leadership techniques. For example, distinguishable from inducing compliance from followers, or unreasonably leveraging power and position authority, was the conception of leadership as "influencing change in the conduct of people"[51]

---

[47] Bass, B.M. 1990. *Handbook of Leadership: Theory, Research and Managerial Applications*, 12, 3rd ed. New York, NY: The Free Press.

[48] Moore, B. 1921. "The May Conference on Leadership." *Personnel Journal* 6, no. 124, pp. 124–28; and Munson, E.L., and A.H. Miller. 1921. *The Management of Men: A Handbook on the Systematic Development of Morale and the Control of Human Behavior*. H. Holt.

[49] Bass, B.M. 1990. *Handbook of Leadership: Theory, Research and Managerial Applications*, 13, 3rd ed. New York, NY: The Free Press.

[50] Id. at p. 15.

[51] Nash, J. 1929. "Leadership." *Phi Delta Kappa* 12, pp. 24–25.

and/or as "the process of influencing the activities of an organized group in its efforts toward goal setting and goal achievement."[52] Related to the emphasis on the use of influence by leaders is the conception of leadership as management "by persuasion and inspiration rather than by the direct or implied threat of coercion."[53] Bass noted that this conception initially found favor among political scientists such as Neustadt, who concluded that leadership among American presidents was often grounded in their powers of persuasion.[54]

In contrast to the emphasis on styles used by leaders to get their followers to take certain actions is the grouping of conceptions that focus on specific acts and behaviors that a person engages in while serving as a leader and attempting to direct and coordinate the work of his or her followers.[55] Bass himself mentioned actions such as "structuring the work relations, praising or criticizing group members, and showing consideration for their welfare and feelings."[56] Related to this conception is the notion of "leadership as the initiation of structure," which is based on the belief that leaders provide the stimulus to structure the behaviors of the members of the group and that leadership itself is the initiation and maintenance of structure in expectation and interaction.[57]

Another important grouping of conceptions focuses on "leadership as a differentiated role": This conception is based on role theory, which

---

[52] Stogdill, R. 1950. "Leadership, Membership and Organization." *Psychological Bulletin* 47, no. 1.

[53] Bass, B.M. 1990. *Handbook of Leadership: Theory, Research and Managerial Applications*, 14, 3rd ed. New York, NY: The Free Press.

[54] Neustadt, R. 1960. *Presidential Power*. New York, NY: Wiley.

[55] See, e.g., Fiedler, F. 1967. *A Theory of Leadership Effectiveness*. New York, NY: McGraw-Hill.

[56] Bass, B.M. 1990. *Handbook of Leadership: Theory, Research and Managerial Applications*, 14, 3rd ed. New York, NY: The Free Press.

[57] Stogdill, R. 1959. *Individual Behaviour and Group Achievement*. New York, NY: Oxford University Press. as quoted in Bass, B.M. 1990. *Handbook of Leadership: Theory, Research and Managerial Applications*, 17, 3rd ed. New York, NY: The Free Press. See also Stogdill, R. 1974. *Handbook of Leadership: A Survey of Theory and Research*, 411. New York, NY: The Free Press, ("Leadership is defined as the initiation and maintenance of structure in expectation and interaction")

asserts that each member of a group occupies a position in the group which is more or less well defined and provides the member with a role to play. Differences among the various roles could be traced to influence, with the distinguishing element of the leader's role being that he or she exerted influence over the other group members—their followers, whose actions were a response to the leader's influence. Bass observed that

> [o]f all the available definitions, the role conception of leadership is most firmly buttressed by research findings … [l]eadership as a differentiated role is required to integrate the various other roles of the group and to maintain unity of action in the group's effort to achieve its goals.[58]

The afore-described conceptions of leadership are not all-inclusive and, in fact, Bass noted that researchers had often attempted to combine some of the elements to cover a larger set of meanings. For example, Bass observed that Jago had defined leadership as "the exercise of non-coercive influence to coordinate the members of an organized group to accomplishing the group's objectives" and had also argued that leadership was "a set of priorities attributed to those who are perceived to use such influences successfully."[59] Tichy and Devanna focused on transformational leadership as emerging from a combination of power and personality and claimed that transformational leaders could be defined as skilled, knowledgeable change agents with power, legitimacy, and energy who were "courageous, value-driven, and able to deal with ambiguity and complexity."[60]

Building on the conception of leadership as an "exercise of influence," Hemphill and Bass described various stages of interaction between leaders

---

[58] Bass, B.M. 1990. *Handbook of Leadership: Theory, Research and Managerial Applications*, 3rd ed, 17. New York, NY: The Free Press.

[59] Jago, A. 1982. "Leadership: Perspectives in Theory and Research." *Management Science* 28, no. 3, pp. 315–36.

[60] Tichy, N., and M. Devanna. 1986. *Transformational Leadership*. New York, NY: Wiley. Summarized in Bass, B.M. 1990. *Handbook of Leadership: Theory, Research and Managerial Applications*, 18, 3rd ed. New York, NY: The Free Press.

and followers, beginning with the leader's initial efforts to change the behaviors of their followers, which they referred to as "attempted leadership."[61] If those efforts actually led to changes among the followers, the creation of change would be considered "successful leadership"; however, leadership would only be deemed "effective" if the followers were reinforced or rewarded for changing their behaviors to suit the requests of the leader.[62] Some have argued that explicit exertion of influence by leaders is discretionary and should be undertaken only with respect to actions that are not otherwise prescribed within the leader's recognized day-to-day managerial roles.[63]

Day and Antonakis

After examining the research and accompanying literature relating to a wide array of theories of organization leadership, Day and Antonakis concluded that a comprehensive definition of leadership must incorporate the most commonly used definitional features: "the leader as person (dispositional characteristics), leader behavior, the effects of a leader, the interaction process between a leader and follower(s), and the importance of context."[64] Day and Antonakis stressed that leadership "is required to direct and guide organizational and human resources toward the strategic

---

[61] Hemphill, J.K. 1949. "The Leader and his Group." *Journal of Educational Research* 28, pp. 225–29, 245–46; and Bass, B.M. 1960. *Leadership, Psychology, and Organizational Behavior*. New York, NY: Harper.

[62] Bass, B.M. 1990. *Handbook of Leadership: Theory, Research and Managerial Applications*, 13, 3rd ed. New York, NY: The Free Press.

[63] Id. at p. 14 (see, for example, Miller, J. 1973. *Structuring/Destructuring Leadership in Open Systems* (Tech. Rep. No. 64). Rochester, NY: University of Rochester, Management Research Centre; and Jacobs, T., and E. Jaques. 1987. "Leadership in Complex Systems." In *Human Productivity Enhancement*, ed. J. Zeidner. New York, NY: Praeger.)

[64] Day, D., and J. Antonakis. 2012. "Leadership: Past, Present and Future." In *The Nature of Leadership*, eds. D. Day and J. Antonakis, 3–25, 5, 2nd ed. Thousand Oaks, CA: Sage Publications (citing also Bass, B.M. 2008. *The Bass Handbook of Leadership: Theory, Research, and Managerial Applications*, 4th ed. New York, NY: Free Press.)

objectives of the organization and ensure that organizational functions are aligned with the external environment."[65] They noted that at the supervisory level, leadership compliments organizational systems by setting group goals and values, maximizing the use of the abilities of group members, and facilitating resolution of problems and conflicts that may arise within the group. In order words, "a leader is a 'completer' who does or gets done whatever is not being adequately handled by the group."[66] At the higher, or executive, level of the organization the leader assumes responsibility for coordinating organizational strategies and activities with the challenges and opportunities that are identified during the leader's scanning and monitoring of organization's external environment.[67]

Levels of Leadership

Zaccaro and Klimoski have argued strongly for careful consideration of organizational levels when studying the roles, functions, and recommended behaviors of organizational leaders.[68] They have endorsed the views of those scholars who have argued that one can observe qualitative shifts in the nature of leadership across organizational leaders and that organizational leadership was moderated by several significant factors such as organizational structure, particularly the organizational level where the leader is operating, the degree of differentiation in function, and the place in organizational space.[69] In the same vein, Muczyk and Adler, after surveying the extensive literature and theories relating to

---

[65] Id. (citing Zaccaro, S. 2001. *The Nature of Executive Leadership: A Conceptual and Empirical Analysis of Success*. Washington, DC: American Psychological Association.)

[66] Id. (citing McGrath, J. 1962. *Leadership Behavior: Some Requirements for Leadership Training*. Washington, DC: U.S. Civil Service Commission, Office of Career Development.)

[67] Id. (citing Katz, D., and R. Kahn. 1978. *The Social Psychology of Organizations*, 2nd ed. New York, NY: Wiley.)

[68] Zaccaro, S., and R. Klimoski. 2001. "The Nature of Organizational Leadership: An Introduction." In *The Nature of Organizational Leadership* (Understanding the Performance Imperatives Confronting Today's Leaders), eds. S. Zaccaro and R. Klimoski, 1–41, 12–13. New York, NY: John Wiley & Sons.

[69] Id. at p. 4.

"leadership," also concluded that the elements of leadership and the recommended behaviors of leaders vary depending on a variety of factors,
including the position of the leader in the hierarchy, the type of business
engaged in by the organization, and the environmental conditions that
the organization is facing.[70] In order to capture these factors and provide
organizational leaders with a way to figure out "what to do and when
to do it," they suggested a framework that included three levels of leadership: "transformational leadership," which was also referred to as "big
leadership," which places the focus on the leader and his or her vision and
direction and largely ignores the influences and opinions of subordinates
when decisions are made about how they are expected to behave; "mid-
range leadership," which they explained to be more "transactional" in
nature because they were "predicated either explicitly or implicitly on the
idea of a 'social compact' between the leader and the subordinates"; and
"small leadership," which involves "little" acts of leadership (e.g., demonstrating knowledge of the job, "walking the talk," fostering listening and
practicing general supervision while allowing subordinates to figure out
the details to achieve results), which can establish the requisite level of
trust between leaders and subordinates that is needed in order to create a
social compact between them that becomes the basis for high productivity and morale within the organization.[71]

---

[70] Muczyk, J., and T. Adler. 2002. "An Attempt at a Consentience Regarding
Formal Leadership." *Journal of Leadership and Organizational Studies* 9, no. 2,
pp. 2–17.

[71] For further discussion of the relationship between organizational level and
leadership roles activities, including a detailed description of each of the levels of
leadership mentioned in the text, see "Leadership Roles and Activities" in "Leadership: A Library of Resources for Sustainable Entrepreneurs" prepared and distributed by the Sustainable Entrepreneurship Project. More information on the
research relating to the "three levels of leadership" can be found in Antonakis,
J., and R. House. 2002. "An Analysis of the Full-Range Leadership Theory: The
Way Forward." In *Transformational and Charismatic Leadership: The Road Ahead*,
eds. B. Avolio and F. Yammarino, 3–34. Amsterdam, Netherlands: JAI; and
Antonakis, J., R. House, J. Rowold, and L. Borgmann. 2010. *A Fuller Full-range
Leadership Theory: Instrumental, Transformational, and Transactional Leadership*,
Unpublished Manuscript. With regard to the second work, the terms "instru-
mental" and "transactional" leadership are similar to the "small" and "mid-range"
leadership, respectively, discussed in the text.

Leadership, Power, and Management

When discussing definitions of leadership it is important to distinguish related concepts of "power" and "management," each of which are often confused with leadership.[72] Day and Antonakis suggested that "power" is rightly seen as "the means leaders have to potentially influence others" and that although power is not leadership it is nonetheless necessary for leaders to have power to be effective in that role.[73] With regard to leadership and management, Day and Antonakis noted that many researchers have come to accept the distinction between leadership as "purpose-driven action" to bring about organizational change or transformation and management as being "objectives driven."[74] Although there are groups of researchers who argue that leaders and managers are different types of individuals,[75] others take the position that "successful leadership also requires successful management, that leadership and management are complementary, but that leadership goes beyond management, and that leadership is necessary for outcomes that exceed expectations."[76]

---

[72] Day, D., and J. Antonakis. 2012. "Leadership: Past, Present and Future." In *The Nature of Leadership*, eds. D. Day and J. Antonakis, 3–25, 5, 2nd ed. Thousand Oaks, CA: Sage Publications.

[73] Id. Day and Antonakis listed several examples of power including referent power, expertise, the ability to reward or punish performance, and the legitimate power of formal position within the organization. See also French, J., and B. Raven, "The Basis of Social Power." In *Group Dynamics: Research and Theory*, eds. D. Cartwright and A. Zander, 259–69, 3rd ed. New York, NY: Harper & Row.

[74] Day, D., and J. Antonakis. 2012. "Leadership: Past, Present and Future." In *The Nature of Leadership*, eds. D. Day and J. Antonakis, 3–25, 5, 2nd ed. Thousand Oaks, CA: Sage Publications.

[75] See, e.g., Zaleznik, A. March-April 1992. "Managers and Leaders: Are they Different?" *Harvard Business Review*, pp. 126–33.

[76] Day, D., and J. Antonakis. 2012. "Leadership: Past, Present and Future" In *The Nature of Leadership*, eds. D. Day and J. Antonakis, 3–25, 5, 2nd ed. Thousand Oaks, CA: Sage Publications. citing Bass, B.M. 1985. *Leadership and Performance Beyond Expectations*. New York, NY: Free Press; Bass, B.M. 1998. *Transformational Leadership: Industrial, Military, and Educational Impact*. Mahwah, NJ: Lawrence Erlbaum; and Bass, B.M., and R. Riggio. 2006. *Transformation Leadership*, 2nd ed. Mahwah, NJ: Lawrence Erlbaum.

Muczyk and Adler argued that given the importance of "leadership" to organizations of all types and sizes it was essential to "attempt to integrate the many disparate concepts and constructs relating to this topic."[77] As part of that process, they took the position that the appropriate approach for laying out the relationship between "leadership" and "management" was the one taken by Mintzberg when he suggested his 10 managerial roles in 1973, namely "… the leadership role is one of 10 managerial roles, although probably the most important one."[78] They rejected suggestions that managerial activities should be subsumed under the broader umbrella of leadership because that would simply lead to "confusion between leadership and the means that a leader employs to obtain compliance from subordinates."[79] They cited Gardner as an example of this approach, noting that he had developed a list of "basic leadership tasks" that included "managing" along with other responsibilities such as envisioning goals, affirming values, motivating, achieving a workable level of unity, explaining, serving as a symbol, representing the group externally, and renewing.[80] They were also critical of Kotter's suggestion that leadership and management were two distinctive, albeit complimentary, systems of action: Leadership focused on coping with "change," which requires providing direction, whereas management focused on coping with "complexity," which requires developing and executing plans.[81] Muczyk and Adler felt that Kotter had made a distinction without a difference and noted not only that "change can be quite complex" but also that one cannot truly be effective in setting and communicating a direction to navigate through a changing environment without also systematically

---

[77] Muczyk, J., and T. Adler. 2002. "An Attempt at a Consentience Regarding Formal Leadership." *Journal of Leadership and Organizational Studies* 9, no. 2, pp. 2–17.

[78] Id.

[79] Id.

[80] Id. (citing Gardner, J. 1987. "The Tasks of Leadership." *New Management* 4, no. 4, pp. 9–14)

[81] Kotter, J. 1996. *Leading Change*. Cambridge, MA: Harvard Business School Press.

creating a plan that can be followed by those that the leader/manager needs to influence and motivate.[82]

Other Definitions and Conceptions of Leadership

Stogdill observed "there are almost as many different definitions of leadership as there are persons who have attempted to define the concept"[83] and by now it should be clear that there is no apparent limit to the creativity of researchers, management consultants, and actual practitioners in devising definitions and conceptions of leadership. Lyne de Ver, as part of her work on the influence of leadership on growth and economic development, noted that although there was an overwhelming consensus that "leadership" was important to the success of organizations and institutions in the private sector, there was still no consensus about how to define leadership, nor was there a model or approach relating to leadership that had garnered the support of scholars and practitioners and which could be used as a basis for assessing the behaviors of leaders or training persons to be more effective leaders. She observed that scholars and practitioners from management and organizational science, psychology, and other related disciplines had been the most prominent contributors to the study of leadership, but that leadership had yet to become a primary concern of those working in political science, economics, or development theory. She commented that one by-product of all this has been that "many of the conceptions of leadership in the literature are Western-oriented, universalist or individualistic" and then went on to present what she referred to as a brief survey of "a representative sample of some of the prevailing conceptions of leadership" that included the following:

Leadership as both an "act" and a "person": "Leadership is both a process and a property. The process of leadership is the use of noncoercive influence to direct and coordinate the activities of the members of an

---

[82] For further discussion of the relationship between leadership and management, see "Management: A Library of Resources for Sustainable Entrepreneurs" prepared and distributed by the Sustainable Entrepreneurship Project.

[83] Stogdill, R. 1974. *Handbook of Leadership: A Survey of Theory and Research*, 7. New York, NY: The Free Press.

organized group toward the accomplishment of group objectives. As a property, leadership is the set of qualities or characteristics attributed to those who are perceived to successfully employ such influence."[84]

Leadership as facilitating creation and achievement of shared goals: "I define leaders as those who help a group create and achieve shared goals. Some try to impose their own goals, others derive them more from the group, but leaders mobilize people to reach those objectives."[85]

Leadership as marshaling collaborative group behavior: According to Dwight Eisenhower, leaders have the ability "to get people to work together, not only because you tell them to do so and enforce your orders but because they instinctively want to do it for you … [y]ou don't lead by hitting people over the head; that's assault, not leadership."[86]

Leadership as transformation of follower "wants" into "needs" specified by the leader: The conceptualization of leadership provided by Burns presumes that followers have primal desires, which may often be bad for or harmful to them, and that it is the role of the leader to transform those desires into needs that are consistent with goals and objectives established by the leader rather than the followers. Burns explained that "[l]eadership over human beings is exercised when persons with certain motives and purposes mobilize, in competition or conflict with others, institutional, political, psychological, and other resources so as to arouse, engage and satisfy the motives of followers."[87]

Upon completion of her survey, Lyne de Ver argued that the prevailing tendency among scholars and practitioners to conceive of leadership in terms of traits and characteristics, roles and behaviors, and styles was inadequate for understanding leadership from a "developmental"

---

[84] Jago, A.G. 1982. "Leadership: Perspectives in Theory and Research." *Management Science* 28, no. 3, pp. 315–36.

[85] Nye, J. 2008. *The Powers to Lead*, New York, NY: Oxford University Press. xi. Nye argued that good and effect leadership required a combination of soft power skills, hard power skills, and "contextual intelligence," whereas Nye described as a leader's ability knowing when to use which combination of soft or hard skills.

[86] Quote appeared in Axelrod, A., and P. Georgescu. 2010. *Eisenhower on Leadership: Ike's Enduring Lessons in Total Victory Management*, 120, 386 vols. San Francisco: Jossey-Bass.

[87] Burns, J. 1978. *Leadership*, 18, New York, NY: Harper Torch Books.

point of view given the neglect of the importance of context and the political nature of leadership. For Lyne de Ver, three guiding principles needed to be acknowledged to construct a definition of leadership for development purposes:

> leadership implies the organization or mobilization of people and resources (economic, political and other) in pursuit of particular ends; leadership must always be understood contextually, occurring within a given indigenous configuration of power, authority and legitimacy, shaped by history, institutions, goals and political culture; and leadership regularly involves forging formal or informal coalitions, vertical or horizontal, of leaders and elites, in order to solve the pervasive collective action problems which largely define the challenges of growth and development.

She then suggested that "developmental leadership" could be defined as

> the process of organizing or mobilizing people and resources in pursuit of particular ends or goals, in given institutional contexts of authority, legitimacy and power (often of a hybrid kind). Achieving these ends, and overcoming the collective action problems which commonly obstruct such achievement, normally requires the building of formal or informal coalitions of interests, elites and organizations, both vertical and horizontal.

Leadership as the exercise of influence has been a popular conception of the term since the beginning of the serious study of leadership, beginning with Nash's view of leadership as the process of "influencing change in the conduct of people" in the late 1920s.[88] Stogdill referred to leadership as "the process of influencing the activities of an organized group in its efforts toward goal setting and goal achievement."[89] Yuki and Van Fleet observed that

---

[88] Nash, J. 1929. "Leadership." *Phi Delta Kappa* 12, pp. 24–25.
[89] Stogdill, R. 1950. "Leadership, Membership and Organization." *Psychological Bulletin* 47, no. 1, p. 1.

[l]eadership is viewed as a process that includes influencing the task objectives and strategies of a group or organization, influencing people in the organization to implement the strategies and achieve the objectives, influencing group maintenance and identification, and influencing the culture of the organization.[90]

Rost called leadership "an influence relationship among leaders and collaborators who intend real changes that reflect their mutual purposes."[91] Northouse described leadership as "a process whereby an individual influences a group of individuals to achieve a common goal."[92]

Zaleznik agreed that leadership involved influencing the thoughts and processes of other people; however, he emphasized that influence typically required the use of power by the leader.[93] Bolden argued that in order for a leader's influence to be effective he or she must succeed in inspiring followers to work toward group goals through personal motivation.[94] The U.S. Department of the Army counseled prospective leaders to engage in influence that involved providing purpose, direction, and motivation.[95] For other scholars, influence was just one of several actions required for a leader to be effective. For example, Van Vugt et al. described leadership as both influencing individuals to contribute to group goals and coordinating the pursuit of those goals,[96] and Yuki observed that leaders must

---

[90] Yukl, G., and D. Van Fleet. 1990. "Theory and Research on Leadership in Organizations." In *Handbook of Industrial and Organizational Psychology*, eds. M. Dunnette and L. Hough, 149, 2nd ed. 3 vols. Palo Alto, CA: Consulting Psychologists Press.

[91] Rost, J.C. 1997. "Moving from Individual to Relationship: A Postindustrial Paradigm of Leadership." *Journal of Leadership & Organizational Studies* 4, no. 4, pp. 3–16.

[92] Northouse, P. 2010. *Leadership: Theory and Practice*, 3, 5th ed. Thousand Oaks, CA: Sage Publications.

[93] Zaleznik, A. May-June 1977. "Managers and Leaders: Are they Different?" *Harvard Business Review* 55, no. 3, p. 67.

[94] Bolden, R. July 2004. "What is Leadership?" *Research Report* 1, 5. Exeter, UK: Leadership South West.

[95] U.S. Army. October 2006. Army Leadership: Competent, Confident and Agile: Field Manual 6–22 Washington, DC: Department of the Army, Glossary 3.

[96] Van Vugt, M., R. Hogan, and R. Kaiser. 2008. "Leadership, Followership, and Evolution: Some Lessons from the Past." *American Psychologist* 63, no. 3, p. 182.

not only influence their followers "to understand and agree about what needs to be done and how to do it" but also design and oversee a "process of facilitating individual and collective efforts to accomplish shared objectives."[97]

Finally, in his effort to provide a sampling of "the many definitions of leadership," Shaver provided additional definitions and conceptions that have not otherwise been covered already in the discussion earlier.[98] He began with the often repeated definition offered by Bennis: "Leadership is a function of knowing yourself, having a vision that is well communicated, building trust among colleagues, and taking effective action to realize your own leadership potential." Also included was Drucker's observation from 1995 that "[l]eadership is the lifting of a man's vision to higher sights, the raising of a man's performance to a higher standard, the building of a man's personality beyond its normal limitations."[99] Other quotes included "leadership should be defined in terms of the ability to build and maintain a group that performs well relative to its competition"[100]; "leadership is the art of mobilizing others to want to struggle for shared aspirations"[101]; "[leadership is]...a process of motivating people to work together collaboratively to accomplish great things"[102]; and "[l]eadership over human beings is exercised when persons with certain motives and purposes mobilize, in competition or conflict with others, institutional, political, psychological, and other resources so as to arouse, engage, and satisfy the motives of followers."[103]

---

[97] Yukl, G. 2010. *Leadership in Organizations*, 8, 7th ed. Upper Saddle River, NJ: Prentice Hall.

[98] Shaver, E. 2018. "The Many Definitions of Leadership." http://ericshaver.com/the-many-definitions-of-leadership/ (accessed December 10, 2018).

[99] Drucker, P.F. 1954. *The Practice of Management*. New York, NY: Harper Business.

[100] Hogan, R., and R.B. Kaiser. 2005. "What We Know about Leadership." *Review of General Psychology* 9, no. 2, p. 169.

[101] Kouzes, J., and B.Z. Posner. 1995. *The Leadership Challenge*, 30. San Francisco: Jossey-Bass.

[102] Vroom, V.H., and A. Jago. 2007. "The Role of Situation in Leadership." *American Psychologist* 62, no. 1, p. 17.

[103] Burns, J. 1978. *Leadership*, 18. New York, NY: Harper & Row.

CHAPTER 2

Leadership Roles and Activities

Introduction

Whereas leaders can be distinguished from managers, leaders nonetheless are responsible for a number of the same functions typically categorized as "managerial" such as setting goals and designing strategic plans to achieve those goals, communicating directives to other members of the organization, overseeing execution of the organizational strategy, and setting guidelines for motivating organizational members and assessing their performance. All leaders, regardless of their position, are engaged in the following core roles and activities provided by the four-factor theory of leadership proposed by Bowers and Seashore: support, in the form of leader behaviors that enhance a subordinate's feelings of personal worth and importance; interaction facilitation, in the form of leader behaviors that encourage organizational members to develop close and mutually satisfying relationships; goal emphasis, in the form of leader behaviors that motivate organizational members to achieve excellent performance and fulfill the goals set for the organization; and work facilitation, in the leader behaviors that support achievement of the organizational performance goals, including activities such as coordinating, planning and scheduling, and providing subordinates with the requisite tools, materials, and technical knowledge necessary for them to do their jobs.[1] In addition, leadership roles and the focus of leader activities vary depending on where he or she is located within the organizational hierarchy. Finally, other factors such as the type of business engaged in by the organization,

---

[1] Muczyk, J.P., and T. Adler. 2002. "An Attempt at a Consentience Regarding Formal Leadership." *Journal of Leadership and Organizational Studies* 9, no. 2, pp. 2–17.

the environmental conditions that the organization is facing, the stage of the organization's development, the leader's role in the launch of the organization (e.g., a "founder"), and the scope of the organization's global business activities will have an influence on the leader's role and the behaviors needed in order for the leader to be effective.[2] The following list lays out various core leadership roles and activities derived from the research and observations described in this chapter.[3]

Core Leadership Roles and Activities

- Selecting and defining goals and objectives for the organization; designing strategic plans to achieve those goals and objectives; and identifying, promoting, and managing changes required to achieve future goals and objectives
- Communicating ideas about their vision for the organization and providing directions to other members of the organization regarding actions to be taken to realize the vision
- Designing and implementing an organizational structure that promotes efficient flow of information and collaboration among members of the organization to develop new products and services and solutions for problems and issues raised by customers
- Overseeing execution of the organizational strategy and establishing procedures for assessing the performance of organizational members
- Implementing human resources management practices that support their vision and provide members of the

---

[2] Id. For discussion of the roles and activities of organizational founders, see "Entrepreneurship: A Library of Resources for Sustainable Entrepreneurs" prepared and distributed by the Sustainable Entrepreneurship Project (www.seproject.org).

[3] See also Dudley, D.D. 2018. This Is Day One: A Practical Guide to Leadership That Matters. New York, NY: Hachette Books.

organization with access to training necessary to maintain and improve the skills required for them to positively participate in the execution of the vision

- Engaging in proactive pursuit and collection of information from internal and external sources and implementation of procedures for efficient analysis and dissemination of relevant information among members of the organization
- Engaging in behaviors that support organizational members and enhance their feelings of personal worth and importance
- Engaging in behaviors that facilitate interaction among organizational members; encourage members to develop close and mutually satisfying relationships; create high-quality teams; and train members of the organization on team building techniques
- Engage in behaviors that motivate organizational members to achieve excellent performance and fulfill the goals set for the organization using a range of techniques such as formal authority, role modeling, delegation of authority, setting specific and challenging goals, and adroit and intelligent use of rewards and punishments
- Engage in behaviors that support achievement of the organizational performance goals, including activities such as coordinating, planning and scheduling, and provid-ing organizational members with the requisite tools, materials, and technical knowledge necessary for them to do their jobs
- Engage in behaviors consistent with service as a steward of the assets, resources, mission, reputation, and legacy of the organization including selection and development of potential future leaders and representing the organization with integrity in the communities in which it operates

Performance Imperatives for Senior Organizational Leaders

Zaccaro and Klimoski surveyed what they referred to as the "four research traditions in leadership" and claimed that it was possible and desirable to identify the most important factors or forces that exist in the operating environment of senior leaders and compiled a list that included the following types of "performance imperatives": cognitive, social, personal, political, technological, financial, and senior staffing.[4] They argued that these performance imperatives, each of which are summarized in the following list and discussed in more detail in the following sections, "define the context of executive leadership action and its effects on organizational effectiveness" and that served as the foundation for a model of leader performance that "specifically links executive characteristics with executive performance requirements and executive performance with organizational success."[5] Zaccaro and Klimoski also asserted that the ability to identify the requisite executive characteristics facilitated the design of effective leader assessment and development programs.

---

[4] Zaccaro, S.J., and R.J. Klimoski. 2002. In *The Nature of Organizational Leadership: An Introduction the Nature of Organizational Leadership* (*Understanding the Performance Imperatives Confronting Today's Leaders*), eds. S. Zaccaro and R. Klimoski, 1–41, 26–30. New York, NY: John Wiley & Sons. Zaccaro and Klimoski commented that their performance "imperatives" were derived "both inductively from reviews of case studies and work description studies [citations omitted] and deductively from several models and perspectives of organizational leadership [citations omitted]." Id. at 5 (text includes detailed list of citations to some of the studies and models reviewed by Zaccaro and Klimoski). See also Zaccaro, S.J., and R.J. Klimoski, eds. 2002. *The Nature of Organizational Leadership: Understanding the Performance Imperatives Confronting Today's Leaders*, 12 vols. Pfeiffer.

[5] Zaccaro, S.J., and R.J. Klimoski. 2002. *In The Nature of Organizational Leadership: An Introduction The Nature of Organizational Leadership* (*Understanding the Performance Imperatives Confronting Today's Leaders*), eds. S. Zaccaro and R. Klimoski, 1–41, 30. New York, NY: John Wiley & Sons.

Checklist of Performance Imperatives for Organizational Leaders

- Does the leader have the requisite *cognitive* skills to effectively scan expansive and relatively unstructured external environments, process and make sense of the information collected from those scanning activities, and use that information to solve problems and forge long-term strategies?
- Does the leader have the *social* skills and competencies that are necessary and appropriate to forge and manage the relationships that are relevant to his or her position within the organizational hierarchy? Senior executives must deal with great social complexity because they are responsible for coordinating and supervising the activities of multiple business units that often have conflicting goals and objectives and must be able to create and maintain large social networks and build up social capital. On the other hand, leaders at the lower levels of the organizational hierarchy are typically faced with more modest social demands because the number of relationships that are responsible is limited to a fewer subordinates and a smaller set of generally homogenous business units.
- Does the leader have the *personal* skills and attributes necessary for timely and skillful execution of activities such as career and reputation management and acquisition of authority and influence? Personal imperatives include the personal values that influence leaders in their decisions about the strategic direction of the organization and/or specific business units, and also play an important role in how executives go about developing and staffing their management teams.
- Does the leader have the requisite *political* skills for acquisition of power, including powers of persuasion; timely and judicious use of power, including the ability to handle and resolve conflicts arising out of attempts to use power;

appropriate application of power sharing; building coalitions within the organization and with external strategic partners; and successfully representing and furthering the interests of the organization in its external environment?

- Does the leader have the skills necessary for coping with the dramatic and sweeping effects that *technological* advances have had on the way organizations operate and compete and the operational environment in which leaders must operate? Leaders must be able to identify the nature and rate of technological change; devise systems and procedures for gathering, distributing, and interpreting information; develop and implement strategies for achieving and maintaining a competitive advantage based on technological advances in production and human resources; and identify and implement strategies that leverage technology to design better control and support systems.

- Does the leader have the skills and tools necessary to successfully develop, implement, monitor, and adjust long- and short-term *financial* goals and objectives and strategies? Leaders of public companies must be particularly sensitive to the tendency to place too much emphasis on short-term thinking in order to generate the financial performance expected and demanded by investors and ignore advice that effective leadership requires a long-term orientation that includes both deliberate strategy and patient vision. The leader's compensation arrangement can have a significant impact on how he or she addresses the financial imperative.

- Does the leader seek and hire candidates for positions at the *senior staffing* level in the organization, including other members of the executive team when the leader is the CEO, who possess, or can easily and quickly acquire, the skills, dispositions, and capabilities required to respond appropriately to the demands associated with the earlier-described performance imperatives? Training and development programs should be designed around each of these imperatives so that prospective leaders can develop the skills that are most relevant to their actual operating environment. Senior leaders must also be adroit at making the right choices about the human resources needed to implement their decisions and ensure the long-term viability of the organization.

Cognitive Imperative—Information Processing and Problem-Solving

Zaccaro and Klimoski used the term "cognitive imperative" to refer to "the complex information processing and problem-solving demands that organizational leaders, particularly executives, need to confront in order to be successful."[6] They commented that these demands arise from the causal factors, many in number and tightly interconnected, that can impact organizational success and from the exponential increases in available data because of technological advances in information processing systems. Executives in particular must have the requisite cognitive skills to effectively scan expansive and relatively unstructured external environments, make sense of the information collected from those scanning activities, and use that information to forge long-term strategies.

Social Imperative—Creation and Management of Relationships

The "social imperative" highlights the behavioral activities and skills that leaders need to have in order to cope with the social complexity in their operating environment, specifically the number, nature, and variability of the relationships that are called upon to forge and manage in order to be successful.[7] Zaccaro and Klimoski argued that the social skills and competencies required of a leader vary depending on the level in the

---

[6] Id. at p. 26.

[7] Id.

organizational hierarchy at which the leader is operating. For example, executives at the top of the hierarchy must deal with great social complexity because they are responsible for coordinating and supervising the activities of multiple business units, many of which have conflicting goals and objectives. Executives must also have social skills to maintain relationships within the organization even as they are driving toward implementation of organizational-wide changes dictated by their decisions regarding the direction of the organization. In order to be successful in these activities, executives must be able to create and maintain large social networks and build up social capital. On the other hand, leaders at the lower levels of the organizational hierarchy are typically faced with more modest social demands than executives because the number of relationships that are responsible is limited to a fewer subordinates and a smaller set of generally homogenous business units.

Personal Imperative—Career and Reputation Management

The "personal imperative" is concerned with "demands on leaders for the timely and skillful execution of such activities as career and reputation management and acquisition of power."[8] Zaccaro and Klimoski note that these issues are particularly important to leaders as they strive to make a personal impact on the organization and successfully move up the organizational ladder to positions of greater influence and authority. Personal imperatives include the personal values that influence leaders in their decisions about the strategic direction of the organization and/or specific business units. In addition, personal imperatives play an important role in how executives go about developing and staffing their management teams.

Political Imperative—Acquisition and Use of Power

The "political imperative" focuses on how leaders deal with the reality that the role of power in their activities necessarily means that they are

---

[8] Id. at p. 27.

operating in a political environment.[9] Zaccaro and Klimoski note that attention to this imperative requires the development of skills related to acquisition of power, timely and judicious use of power, appropriate application of power sharing, and building coalitions. In order to be politically successful, leaders must develop and apply techniques of persuasion and learn how to handle and resolve conflicts arising out of attempts to use and/or acquire power. Executives must also have the political acumen to skillfully and successfully represent and further the interests of the organization in its external environment, particularly in the interorganizational relationships that are forged with strategic alliance partners, regulators, and members of the community in which the organization operates.

Technological Imperative—Management of Technological Change

The "technological imperative" recognizes the dramatic and sweeping effects that technological advances have had on the way organizations operate and compete and, of course, the operational environment in which leaders must operate.[10] Technology generates more information and this leads to both opportunities and challenges. For example, among the nonroutine problems confronting leaders coping with the technological imperative are identifying the nature and rate of technological change, devising systems and procedures for gathering and distributing information, interpreting the massive amounts of data that are now available, and developing and implementing strategies for achieving and maintaining a competitive advantage based on technological advances in production and human resources.[11] In addition, leaders need to consider how information technology changes their strategic decision processes and how such technology can be used to design better control and support systems.

---

[9] Id. at pp. 27–28.
[10] Id. at pp. 28–29.
[11] Id. at p. 9.

Financial Imperative—Long- and Short-Term Strategic Planning

Senior leaders dealing with financial imperatives must continuously grapple with developing, implementing, monitoring, and adjusting long- and short-term strategies. In fact, Zaccaro and Klimoski observed that the financial imperative "is perhaps the most fundamental source of pressures on senior organizational leaders," particularly among leaders of large corporations with publicly traded securities that are closely scrutinized by the investment community.[12] One of the biggest challenges is the inclination to engage in short-term thinking with respect to strategies on matters such as mergers and acquisitions in order to generate the financial performance expected and demanded by investor and ignore the advice of theorists that effective leadership requires a long-term orientation that includes both deliberate strategy and patient vision. The problem is exacerbated by executive compensation policies that are tilted toward rewards for meeting short-term performance milestones.

Senior Staffing Imperative—Building and Nurturing Senior Leadership

Zaccaro and Klimoski described the "senior staffing imperative" as representing the pressures on the organization to respond appropriately to the demands on its senior leaders represented by the earlier-described imperatives when making decisions regarding selection, training and development, and assessment of those leaders.[13] In other words, Zaccaro and Klimoski argued that the focus of staffing decisions for senior organizational positions should be on identifying individuals who possess, or can easily and quickly acquire, the skills, dispositions, and capabilities required to cope with the performance imperatives that they had described. In addition, training and development programs should be designed around each of these imperatives so that prospective leaders can develop the skills that are most relevant to their actual operating

---

[12] Id. at p. 29.
[13] Id. at pp. 29–30.

environment. Another important aspect of the senior staffing imperative is how the most senior leader, the "CEO," selects and interacts with the members of his or her executive team. Among other things, senior leaders must be able to support the pursuit of their decisions regarding organizational purposes by making the right choices about the human resources needed to implement those decisions.

Organizational Level and Leadership Roles and Activities

Zaccaro and Klimoski have argued strongly for careful consideration of organizational levels when studying the roles, functions, and recommended behaviors of organizational leaders.[14] They have endorsed the views of those scholars who have argued that one can observe qualitative shifts in the nature of leadership across organizational leaders and that organizational leadership was moderated by several significant factors such as organizational structure, particularly the organizational level where the leader is operating; the degree of differentiation in function; and the place in organizational space.[15] For support of their arguments, Zaccaro and Klimoski referred to the "patterns of organizational leadership" that Katz and Kahn associated with three different levels in the organizational hierarchy. First of all, operations at the lower levels of the organizational hierarchy generally flow almost automatically through the administrative use of existing organizational structures and any problems that may arise are usually resolved using existing organizational mechanisms and procedures. In other words, because organizational activity at these levels is so institutionalized there are few situations that present opportunities for leadership action. Second, leaders at the middle levels of the organizational hierarchy do become involved in the embellishment and operationalization of formal structural elements; however, the success of leaders at these levels depends primarily on their ability to work effectively with both superiors and subordinates and their human relations skills. Finally, senior leaders at the top of the organizational hierarchy

---

[14] Id. at pp. 12–13.

[15] Id. at p. 4.

are most concerned with overall policy formulations (i.e., organizational strategies) and designing the organizational structure that is most appropriate for the effective and successful pursuit of such policies.[16]

In the same vein, Muczyk and Adler observed that organizations face three fundamental challenges: (1) developing and articulating the goals and purposes of the organization (i.e., just what is the organization attempting to accomplish); (2) creating an organizational environment in which employees are able to figure out what is required of them and then do their activities well; and (3) making a compelling case to each employee as to why he or she should get excited about working for the organization.[17] They noted that meeting these challenges, and achieving the desired financial and operational "results" of the organization, is the job of the various "leaders" within the organization, not only the person sitting at the top of the organizational hierarchy but also managers, supervisors, and others toiling at all levels of that hierarchy. After surveying the extensive literature and theories relating to "leadership," Muczyk and Adler also concluded that the elements of leadership and the recommended behaviors of leaders vary depending on a variety of factors, including the position of the leader in the hierarchy, the type of business engaged in by the organization, and the environmental conditions that

---

[16] Id. (citing Katz, D., and R.L. Kahn. 1978. *The Social Psychology of Organizations*, 2nd ed. New York, NY: Wiley.) Other researchers that have suggested models that incorporate differences across levels of organizational leadership include Jacobs, T.O., and E. Jaques. 1987. "Leadership in Complex Systems." In *Human Productivity Enhancement*, ed. J. Zeidner. New York, NY: Praeger; Mumford, M.D., S.J. Zaccaro, F.D. Harding, E. Fleishman, and R. Reiter-Palmon. 1993. *Cognitive and Temperament Predictors of Executive Ability: Principles for Developing Leadership Capacity*. Alexandria, VA: U.S. Army Research Institute for the Behavioral and Social Sciences; and Bentz, V.J. 1987. *Explorations of Scope and Scale: The Critical Determinant of High-Level Effectiveness*. Greensboro, NC: Center for Creative Leadership.

[17] Muczyk, J.P., and T. Adler. 2002. "An Attempt at a Consentience Regarding Formal Leadership." *Journal of Leadership and Organizational Studies* 9, no. 2, pp. 2–17 (citing Huey, J. February 21, 1994. "The New Post-Heroic Leadership." *Fortune*, pp. 42–45).

the organization is facing.[18] In order to capture these factors and provide organizational leaders with a way to figure out "what to do and when to do it," they suggested a framework discussed in the following sections that included three levels of leadership: "transformational leadership," which was also referred to as "big leadership," "mid-range leadership," and "small leadership."[19]

Levels of Leadership

- **Big (Transformational) Leadership:** Senior leaders at the top of the organizational hierarchy are most concerned with overall policy formulations (i.e., organizational strategies) and designing the organizational structure that is most appropriate for the effective and successful pursuit of such policies.
- **Mid-Range Leadership:** Leaders at the middle levels of the organizational hierarchy do become involved in the embellishment and operationalization of formal structural elements; however, the success of leaders at these levels depends primarily on their ability to work effectively with both superiors and subordinates and their human relations skills.

---

[18] Muczyk, J.P., and T. Adler. 2002. "An Attempt at a Consentience Regarding Formal Leadership." *Journal of Leadership and Organizational Studies* 9, no. 2, pp. 2–17.

[19] For further discussion of the "three levels of leadership," see Antonakis, J., and R.J. House. 2002. "An Analysis of the Full-range Leadership Theory: The Way Forward." In *Transformational and Charismatic Leadership: The Road Ahead*, eds. B. Avolio and F. Yammarino, 3–34. Amsterdam, Netherlands: JAI; and Antonakis, J., R.J. House, J. Rowold, and L. Borgmann. 2010. *A Fuller Full-Range Leadership Theory: Instrumental, Transformational, and Transactional Leadership.* Unpublished Manuscript. With regard to the second work, the terms "instrumental" and "transactional" leadership are similar to the "small" and "mid-range" leadership, respectively, discussed in the text.

- **Small Leadership:** Operations at the lower levels of the organizational hierarchy generally flow almost automatically through the administrative use of existing organizational structures and any problems that may arise are usually resolved using existing organizational mechanisms and procedures—in other words, because organizational activity at these levels is institutionalized and there are few situations that present opportunities for leadership action.

Transformational Leadership

Transformational leadership has been referred to as "a set of behaviors that transform followers' commitment and energy beyond the minimum levels prescribed by the organization."[20] Bass, one of the most well-known proponents of "transformational leadership," has written that transformational leaders influence their subordinates in three significant ways: (1) increasing their awareness of the importance of their tasks and the need to perform those tasks well; (2) making them aware of their own needs for personal growth, development, and accomplishment; and (3) motivating them to strive for the "good of the whole" as opposed to simply pursuing their own personal agendas.[21] Muczyk and Adler questioned whether Bass' concept of "transformational leadership" actually delineated a meaningful distinction from things that all types of leaders should do and noted that the attributes described by Bass had previously been associated with successful leadership by numerous investigators and

---

[20] Muczyk, J.P., and D. Holt. May 2008. "Toward a Cultural Contingency Model of Leadership." *Journal of Leadership & Organizational Studies* 14, no. 4, pp. 277–86, 280. (citing Podsakoff, P.M., S.B. MacKenzie, R.H. Moorman, and R. Fetter. 1990. "Transformational Leader Behaviors and their Effects on Followers' Trust in Leader, Satisfaction, and Organizational Citizenship Behaviors." *Leadership Quarterly* 1, no. 2, pp. 107–42).

[21] Muczyk, J.P., and T. Adler. 2002. "An Attempt at a Consentience Regarding Formal Leadership." *Journal of Leadership and Organizational Studies* 9, no. 2, pp. 2–17. (citing Bass, B.M. 1985. *Leadership and Performance Beyond Expectations*, New York, NY: Free Press.)

that transformational leadership as Bass described it could be found at all organizational levels.[22] In response, Muczyk and Adler suggested that "… transformational leadership is "big leadership," and an operational definition of transformational leader includes four ingredients—inspirational vision, dynamic personality (charisma), crisis situation, and dramatic acts to bring about the transformation …."[23]

Muczyk and Adler emphasized that the traditional notion of "transformational leadership" assumed that leaders were able to influence their subordinates "through inspiration created by the interaction of vision and charisma and enabled by position power."[24] They noted that "vision" could be distinguished from the formal, long-term strategic plan that is developed through the assessment of organizational strengths and weaknesses and opportunities and threats in the organizational environment. Similarly, Kirkpatrick and Locke observed that "the core job of a leader … is to create a vision—a concept of what the organization should be."[25] Creating the vision is not sufficient, however, and a leader must also be able to communicate this vision to his or her followers and, finally, participate in the development and implementation of general strategies for achieving the vision (i.e., a "strategic vision"). Vision-setting supported by

---

[22] Muczyk, J., and T. Adler. 2002. "An Attempt at a Consentience Regarding Formal Leadership." *Journal of Leadership and Organizational Studies* 9, no. 2, pp. 2–17. See also Conger, J.C., and R. Kanungo, eds. 1988. *Charismatic Leadership: The Elusive Factor in Organizational Effectiveness.* San Francisco: Jossey-Bass; Conger, J.A. 1989. *The Charismatic Leader: Behind the Mystique of Exceptional Leadership.* San Francisco: Jossey-Bass.

[23] Muczyk, J.P., and T. Adler. 2002. "An Attempt at a Consentience Regarding Formal Leadership." *Journal of Leadership and Organizational Studies* 9, no. 2, pp. 2–17. Further information on transformational leadership is available from a number of sources including Cherry, K. 2018. "Transformational Leadership: A Closer Look at the Effects of Transformational Leadership." November 19, 2018. https://verywellmind.com/what-is-transformational-leadership-2795313; and https://legacee.com/transformational_leadership/

[24] Muczyk, J.P., and T. Adler. 2002. "An Attempt at a Consentience Regarding Formal Leadership." *Journal of Leadership and Organizational Studies* 9, no. 2, pp. 2–17.

[25] Kirkpatrick, S., and E. Locke. 1991. "Leadership: Do Traits Matter?" *Academy of Management Executive* 5, no. 2, pp. 48–60, 56.

corresponding appropriate values, as well as coping with uncertainty and ambiguity and fostering "creative destruction," is also an integral leadership principle for advocates of the "new sciences" approach to leadership actions and development.[26]

In order to fulfill their responsibilities with respect to the organizational "vision," Kirkpatrick and Locke suggest that leaders must engage in several key activities[27]:

- *Communicating*: Leaders must communicate their ideas about their vision for the organization to the followers and this can be done using a variety of tools and methods such as inspirational speeches, written messages, appeals to shared values, and, perhaps most importantly, acting as a role model with behaviors that are consistent with the vision.[28]

- *Structuring*: Leaders must design and implement an organizational structure that promotes the most efficient flow of information downward, upward, and diagonally. Particular attention should be placed on making sure that information from customers regarding their needs and opinions of product quality and service is quickly collected, disseminated, analyzed, and incorporated into product development and customer service.

- *Selecting and Training*: Human resources management practices should support the vision and ensure that new

---

[26] Fairholm, M. 2004. "A New Sciences Outline for Leadership Development." *The Leadership and Organization Development Journal* 25, no. 4, p. 369. See also Wheatley, M. 2006. Leadership and the New Science: Discovering Order in a Chaotic World, 3rd ed. San Francisco: Berrett-Koehler Publishers. For further discussion, see "History and Evolution of Leadership Studies" prepared and distributed by the Sustainable Entrepreneurship Project (www.seproject.org).

[27] The following discussion of key leader activities with respect to pursuit and achievement of their organizational vision is adapted from Kirkpatrick, S.A., and E.A. Locke. 1991. "Leadership: Do Traits Matter?" *Academy of Management Executive* 5, no. 2, pp. 48–60, 56–58.

[28] On leadership communications, see Booher, D. 2017. *Communicate Like a Leader: Connecting Strategically to Coach, Inspire, and Get Things.* DonePaperback–Oakland, CA: Berrett-Koehler Publishers.

hires have the traits and skills necessary to accept and implement the vision and that all employees have continuous access to the training necessary to maintain and improve the skills required for them to positively participate in the execution of the vision.

- *Motivating*: Kirkpatrick and Locke argue that leaders cannot implement their visions on their own and need the support and assistance of others throughout the organization. In order to gather the necessary support, leaders must be able to motivate their followers using a range of procedures such as formal authority, role modeling, building subordinate self-confidence, delegation of authority, setting specific and challenging goals, and enforcing pursuit of the vision through reasonable, fair, and intelligent use of rewards and punishments.

- *Managing Information*: One of the most important roles of the leader is managing information needed for the organization to pursue the vision and survive and thrive in its operating environment. Leaders proactively seek and collect information from sources throughout the organization, through both formal reporting mechanisms and simple "listening," and from outside the organization. In addition, the leader takes responsibility for disseminating information throughout the organization so that subordinates understand why the leader is making certain decisions and how their activities fit into the pursuit of the goals and objectives associated with the vision.[29]

- *Team Building*: Realizing the goals and objectives of the vision requires collaboration among large groups of people, often situated in widely dispersed areas of the organizational structure. Accordingly, leaders must focus on building effective

---

[29] Kirkpatrick and Locke astutely observe that leaders must be "efficient" when disseminating information, just as they are with other activities, and that they must take the time to organize information in a manner that is most useful to subordinates and which does not overwhelm them. Kirkpatrick, S., and E. Locke. 1991. "Leadership: Do Traits Matter?" *Academy of Management Executive* 5, no. 2, pp. 48–60, 57.

teams, starting at the top with his or her own team of senior managers[30] and then proceeding downward and across the organizational structure. The decisions made regarding hiring, training, and motivating have a big influence on the quality of teams throughout the organization, and people everywhere should be coached on team building so that they have the tools to create and operate effective teams on their own.

- *Promoting Change and Innovation*: Because the leader's vision is a "desired future state" for the organization, he or she must be adroit at identifying, promoting, and managing the changes necessary to reach his or her goals for the future. Kirkpatrick and Locke note that being a "change agent" requires constant restructuring, continual retraining of the workforce to develop new skills, setting and pursuing specific goals for innovation and improvement and rewarding innovation, encouraging information flow, and emphasizing responsiveness to customer needs and concerns.

Kirkpatrick and Locke argued leaders cannot execute their vision for the organization on their own and must be able to communicate that vision to their followers and motivate them to work toward that vision with enthusiasm, commitment, and compliance.[31] Kirkpatrick and Locke went on to identify and briefly describe the following suggested procedures that leaders can use in order to motivate their followers[32]:

---

[30] Team building among the members of the senior management team is an important subject that is discussed in more detail in Hambrick, D.C. 1987. "The Top Management Team: Keys to Strategic Success." *California Management Review* 30, no. 1, pp. 1–20.

[31] Kirkpatrick, S., and E. Locke. 1991. "Leadership: Do Traits Matter?" *Academy of Management Executive* 5, no. 2, pp. 48–60, 57. Other leader activities required to implement the leader's vision for the organization are discussed elsewhere in this chapter.

[32] Id. For further discussion of motivation in the workplace, see "Human Resources: A Library of Resources for Sustainable Entrepreneurs" prepared and distributed by the Sustainable Entrepreneurship Project (www.seproject.org).

- *Formal authority*: Leaders can, and should, constructively use the power and authority associated with their formal position in the organizational hierarchy. Peters was quoted for his advice to leaders that they "[j]ust ask for it"[33] and Kirkpatrick and Locke admonished leaders to be direct and clear with their orders and instructions.

- *Role modeling*: Although exercising formal authority is important, leaders must do more than simply tell their followers what to do—they should be prepared to serve as role models for the desired and expected behaviors.[34] Kirkpatrick and Locke illustrate this principle by noting that leaders pushing for a customer orientation among followers must be consistently and visibly involved in talking with customers themselves.

- *Building self-confidence*: In order for followers to be truly helpful to the leader in sharing the burdens of pursuing the organizational vision, they must be adequately trained and supported so that they have the requisite self-confidence to carry out their designated roles. Building a self-confident workforce begins with recruitment, continues with training, and is maintained by decision-making processes that "empower" workers to act on their own, consistent with the organization's goals and best interests.[35]

- *Delegating authority*: Recruitment, training, and the resultant experience not only build self-confidence, but should

---

[33] See. Peters, T., and K. Rodabaugh. 1988. *Thriving on Chaos: Handbook for a Management Revolution*. New York, NY: Harper Paperbacks.

[34] Kirkpatrick and Locke cited Bandura for the observation that people may learn as much or more by observing models than from the consequences of their own actions. See Bandura, A. 1986. *Social Foundations of Thought and Action: A Social Cognitive Theory*. Englewood Cliffs, NJ: Prentice-Hall.

[35] Kirkpatrick and Locke referenced Conger's observation that "empowerment" is the process of strengthening subordinates' belief in their capabilities. See Conger, J.A., and R.N. Kanungo. 1988. *Charismatic Leadership: The Elusive Factor in Organizational Effectiveness*. San Francisco: Jossey-Bass.

facilitate effective delegation of authority downward in the organizational hierarchy so that leaders can concentrate on "big picture" issues without having to need to constantly meddle in the details. Kirkpatrick and Locke noted that "[g]iving autonomy and responsibility to employees also creates empowerment" and pointed out that Manz and Sims argued that delegating authority actually enhances the power of leaders by building a strong and committed team below them.[36]

- *Setting specific and challenging goals*: Effective leaders establish specific and challenging goals for subordinates. Kirkpatrick and Locke argue that the use of challenging goals reinforces empowerment by demonstrating confidence in the abilities and commitment of subordinates; however, goal setting must be accompanied by regular feedback based on objective tracking of progress toward the specified goals (i.e., performance measurement). In addition, the groundwork should be laid for employee commitment to the goals through the various steps such as role modeling, training, and delegation of authority.[37]

- *Adroit and intelligent use of rewards and punishments*: Effective leaders use the rewards and punishments available to them by virtue of their formal authority as a means for ensuring that followers respect and embrace the organizational vision and achieve the reasonable goals that have been established for them. Rewards and punishments not only have a direct impact on the particular follower, but also send a message to others in the organization. With respect to rewards, Kirkpatrick and Locke specifically note that "[r]ewards may include

---

[36] Kirkpatrick, S.A., and E.A. Locke. 1991. "Leadership: Do Traits Matter?" *Academy of Management Executive* 5, no. 2, pp. 48–60, 57. (citing Manz, C., and J. Sims. 1989. *Superleadership: Leading Others to Lead Themselves.* New York, NY: Prentice Hall.)

[37] For evidence and further information on goal setting, see Locke, E., and G. Latham. 1990. *A Theory of Goal Setting and Task Performance.* Englewood Cliffs, NJ: Prentice Hall.

pay raises, promotions and awards, as well as recognition and praise ... [e]ffective leaders do not just reward achievement, they celebrate it."[38]

Mid-Range Leadership

In addition to their critiques of various aspects of the concept of "transformational leadership," Muczyk and Adler argued that it was important to remember that the need for "leadership" was not confined to the top of the organizational hierarchy but was required "practically everywhere" within the organization.[39] As such, they felt that more emphasis needed to be placed on understanding what they referred to as "mid-range leadership," which they explained to be more "transactional" in nature because they were "predicated either explicitly or implicitly on the idea of a "social compact" between the leader and the subordinates." The transactional exchange in this context begins with the construction of an agenda by the leaders followed by "bargaining" with the subordinates until the subordinates agree to comply with the agenda, perhaps in a modified form, because compliance has "something in it" for both sides. In other words, as Muczyk and Adler point out, this type of leadership "involves both downward and upward influences."[40] In contrast, "big leadership" is not really an alliance of equals because the focus is on the leader and his or

---

[38] Kirkpatrick, S.A., and E.A. Locke. 1991. "Leadership: Do Traits Matter?" *Academy of Management Executive* 5, no. 2, pp. 48–60, 57.

[39] Muczyk, J.P., and T. Adler. 2002. "An Attempt at a Consentience Regarding Formal Leadership." *Journal of Leadership and Organizational Studies* 9, no. 2, pp. 2–17 (citing Muczyk, J., and B. Reimann. March-April 1987. "The Case for Directive Leadership." *The Academy of Management Executive* 1, no. 3, pp. 301–11); and Muczyk, J.P., and R. Steel. 1998. "Leadership Style and the Turnaround Executive." *Business Horizons*, pp. 39–46.

[40] Muczyk, J.P., and T. Adler. 2002. "An Attempt at a Consentience Regarding Formal Leadership." *Journal of Leadership and Organizational Studies* 9, no. 2, pp. 2–17. (citing Muczyk, J.P., and B. Reimann. 1987. "The Case for Directive Leadership." *The Academy of Management Executive* 1, no. 3, pp. 301–11.); and Muczyk, J., and R. Steel. March-April 1998. "Leadership Style and the Turnaround Executive." *Business Horizons*, 39–46.

her vision and direction, and the influences and opinions of subordinates are largely ignored when decisions are made about how they are expected to behave.[41]

Muczyk and Adler noted that there were a number of theories of "mid-range leadership" that have attempted to describe the dynamics of exchange relationships between leaders and their subordinates and commented that work still needed to be done to identify the "constituent components of leadership," or the "crucial leadership dimensions," and sort out which of those were "normative" (i.e., "universal") and which were "situational." They suggested that a good place to start was the mid-range leadership theory proposed by Muczyk and Reimann based on observations of leadership behavior in North America, which had the following five leadership dimensions[42]:

1. Consideration: Concern for people; good human relations; and treating subordinates with dignity, courtesy, and respect
2. Concern for production: Emphasis on challenging goals; achievement orientation; and high standards

---

[41] Muczyk, J., and T. Adler. 2002. "An Attempt at a Consentience Regarding Formal Leadership." *Journal of Leadership and Organizational Studies* 9, no. 2, pp. 2–17. (citing Porter, L.W., R.W. Allen, and H.L. Angle. 1981. "The Politics of Upward Influence in Organizations." In *Research in Organizational Behavior*, eds. L. Cummings and B. Staw, 109–49, 3 vols. Greenwich, CT: JAI Press.)

[42] Muczyk, J.P., and T. Adler. 2002. "An Attempt at a Consentience Regarding Formal Leadership." *Journal of Leadership and Organizational Studies* 9, no. 2, pp. 2–17. (citing Muczyk, J., and B. Reimann. 1987. "The Case for Directive Leadership." *The Academy of Management Executive* 1, no. 3, pp. 301–11). Muczyk and Adler acknowledged that their theory of "mid-range leadership" was also influenced by the works of various scholars, including Fiedler, F. 1967. *A Theory of Leadership Effectiveness*. New York, NY: McGraw-Hill; Hersey, P., and K. Blanchard. 1982. *Management of Organizational Behavior*, 4th ed. Englewood Cliffs, NJ: Prentice-Hall; House, R.J. 1971. "A Path Goal Theory of Leader Effectiveness." *Administrative Science Quarterly* 16, pp. 3–24; Blake, R., and J. Mouton. 1964. *The Managerial Grid*. Houston: Gulf Publishing Co.; and Oesch, T. February 26, 2018. "Effective Leadership Training for Mid-Level Leaders." https://trainingindustry.com/articles/leadership/effective-leadership-training-for-mid-level-leaders/

3. Incentive for performance: Creating the strongest performance reward connection that is permitted within the applicable organizational constraints

4. Participatory or democratic leadership: Degree to which subordinates are involved in making significant day-to-day, work-related decisions, including goal setting

5. Direction: Amount of follow-up or directive behavior associated with execution of a decision that has been made or attainment of a goal that has been established

Muczyk and Adler argued that in order to be "effective," leaders needed to score well on the first three dimensions (i.e., consideration, concern for production, and incentive for performance), regardless of the situational context and that the "prescription for these dimensions is a normative one."[43] They claimed that research confirmed that those firms that were "well-run" placed a premium on "sound human relations, high performance expectations and rewards tied to accomplishment." However, Muczyk and Adler went on to say that high scores on the first three dimensions were not all that was needed for leaders to be effective and that they also needed to display the appropriate mix of participatory and directive behavior for a given situation. In other words, the last two dimensions were "situational" and this meant that effective leaders were those persons who were able to read and understand the internal and external environment at a particular time and adapt their behavior

---

[43] Muczyk, J.P., and D. Holt. May 2008. "Toward a Cultural Contingency Model of Leadership." *Journal of Leadership & Organizational Studies* 14, no. 4, pp. 277–86, 278. (citing Muczyk, J., and T. Adler. 2002. "An Attempt at a Consentience Regarding Formal Leadership." *Journal of Leadership and Organizational Studies*, 9, no. 2, pp. 2–17.) It should be noted, however, that Muczyk and Holt observed that even among these "universals," differences could be found based on the cultural profile of the society within which the leader was acting. Muczyk, J.P., and D. Holt. May 2008. "Toward a Cultural Contingency Model of Leadership." *Journal of Leadership & Organizational Studies* 14, no. 4, pp. 277–86, 282–83. For further discussion of the impact of societal culture on these leadership dimensions, see "Cross-Cultural Leadership Studies" prepared and distributed by the Sustainable Entrepreneurship Project (www.seproject.org).

accordingly by choosing from among four "leadership types" generated by combining the extremes of the "participation" and "direction" dimensions in the Muczyk and Reimann model: directive autocrat, permissive autocrat, directive democrat, and permissive democrat.[44]

Small Leadership

Muczyk and Adler, along with others, have observed that the typical focus of transformational and transactional leadership activities is often problems and activities that are so large, complex, and daunting that leaders can often be so overwhelmed that "a paralysis ensues with respect to goal-directed behavior."[45] McGill and Slocum have written that there are generally two reactions from persons in a leadership role when they are confronted with an "awesome challenge" or "overwhelming task":

> [t]he leadership challenge is so important and its magnitude so daunting that there is no way we can act upon it ... [and] ... [w]hatever action we can take is so insignificant as to have no appreciable impact on resolving the issues facing my organization.[46]

---

[44] Muczyk, J., and T. Adler. 2002. "An Attempt at a Consentience Regarding formal Leadership." *Journal of Leadership and Organizational Studies* 9, no. 2, pp. 2–17. Muczyk and Adler noted that there might be confusion as to why a distinction is made between "participation" and "direction"; however, they explain that the concepts are complementary and that it is possible and realistic to distinguish between the process that a leader uses to make decisions about goals and objectives and the leader's style with respect to managing and overseeing how the decision is actually executed by subordinates (i.e., the amount of delegation by the leader), regardless of the level of participation that the subordinates had in making the decision in the first place. These distinctions become clearer in the descriptions of the four leadership types, or styles, elsewhere in this library.

[45] Muczyk, J.P., and T. Adler. 2002. "An Attempt at a Consentience Regarding Formal Leadership." *Journal of Leadership and Organizational Studies* 9, no. 2, pp. 2–17.

[46] McGill, M.E., and J.W. Slocum, Jr. 1998. "A Little Leadership, Please?" *Organizational Dynamics*. Winter.

The response of leaders in this situation according to Kotter, as well as other researchers, should be "planning for and creating short-term wins" so that people within the organization do not lose hope, give up and dig in their heels, and resist any type of change that would improve the situation for the organization.[47] In the eyes of Muczyk and Adler, "small successes along the way toward an overarching goal sustains momentum so essential to getting large tasks accomplished in a satisfactory manner by reinforcing commitment and boosting motivation."[48]

Recognizing the importance of, and pursuing, these "small wins" has been referred to as "small leadership" and it has been observed that this type of leadership is particularly significant near the bottom of the organizational hierarchy where subordinates are asked to complete tasks and activities that are small, yet vital, steps on the way to effective implementation of the two larger leadership dimensions. Muczyk and Adler observed that "there are countless "little" acts of leadership" and suggested that the concept could be illustrated by the model created by McGill and Slocum that proposed the following four categories of "little" acts of leadership which they argued created the requisite level of trust between leaders and subordinates to create a social compact between them that becomes the basis for high productivity and morale within the organization[49]:

- Knowledge of the job: According to McGill and Slocum, leaders at all levels in the organization must have "a thorough knowledge of [their] job, not only in the details of the task, but in a grasp of the total situation as it is and as it may develop."[50] Knowledge of their work is essential for a leader to be able to carry out their responsibilities with respect to

---

[47] Kotter, J.P. March/April 1995. "Leading Change: Why Transformation Efforts Fail." *Harvard Business Review*, pp. 59–67.

[48] Muczyk, J., and T. Adler. 2002. "An Attempt at a Consentience Regarding Formal Leadership." *Journal of Leadership and Organizational Studies* 9, no. 2, pp. 2–17.

[49] Id. citing McGill, M.E., and J. Slocum. 1988. "A Little Leadership, Please?" *Organizational Dynamics*. Winter.

[50] Id.

training their subordinates, answering technical questions, improving the methods and processes used within the organization, and ensuring that the outputs of the organization meet or exceed the desired quality levels.

- "Say and do": In order to be seen and perceived as a leader, one must continuously act in ways that are consistent with the published and celebrated values of the organization. In other words, a leader must be able to "walk the talk" in order to maintain his or her credibility. In addition, organizational practices created by the leaders must be consistent with organizational values. For example, if performance, quality, and customer services are highlighted as organizational values, subordinates must be recognized and rewarded for actions that support those values. Similarly, if an organization claims that employee involvement is important it had better make sure that employees are included in making decisions and setting goals and that information is made available to employees to allow them to be valuable participants in the decision-making process. Another example is the need for executives, managers, and supervisors to back up their pronouncements about "employees being their most important asset" by creating an employee-centered environment in which employees truly do feel valued and are comfortable approaching leaders about their work-related and personal problems.[51]

- Foster listening: Good listening is one of the most important elements of "small" leadership, and leaders must take steps to convince their employees that they are listening to employee opinions and concerns. McGill and Slocum recommend that organizations implement programs to make their leaders

---

[51] Muczyk, J.P., E.B. Schwartz, and E. Smith. 1984. *Principles of Supervision: First-and Second-Level Management*. Columbus, OH: Charles E. Merrill Publishing Co. Interestingly, this guidance includes elements of the "paternalistic" leadership or management style frequently discussed in the literature and especially associated with organizations grounded in Asian societal cultures.

"better listeners" and that each leader seek out ways to improve their listening skills on their own.

- Context of choice: McGill and Slocum suggest that once employees are properly motivated and trained, it is best for managers and supervisors to use "general supervision" to oversee day-to-day activities, which means that they will "give directions in a general way, with explanations and suggestions, but leave details of method and sequence to the worker." In other words, a general supervisor is somewhat like the "permissive" leader in the Muczyk/Reimann model in that he or she is more concerned about results than about the way in which the results were achieved. General supervision is a cost-effective form of job enrichment, because it requires no changes in technology or work methods and makes employees more self-reliant and prepares them to take on more responsibility. In addition, general supervision allows the manager or supervisor to focus on other functions associated with his or her position.

Muczyk and Adler commented that there are more opportunities for leaders to share the responsibilities associated with the leadership process as one moves farther down the organizational hierarchy.[52] For example, "knowledge of the job" and "context of choice" in the McGill/Slocum model overlap with the leader's responsibilities with respect to "work facilitation" mentioned elsewhere in this chapter and effective "small leadership" includes assigning certain work facilitation activities—coordinating and scheduling, for example, to subordinates. In addition, other aspects of "work facilitation," such as providing subordinates with the necessary technical knowledge, can be done most efficiently as part of the "knowledge of job" component of "small leadership"—in other words, by supervisors working daily with their subordinates on achieving a continuous stream of incremental improvements.

---

[52] Muczyk, J., and T. Adler. 2002. "An Attempt at a Consentience Regarding Formal Leadership." *Journal of Leadership and Organizational Studies* 9, no. 2, pp. 2–17.

Cross-Cultural Competencies for Global Leaders

Leadership is an essential element of any organizational effort to set and achieve meaningful goals and objectives and support the aspirations of organizational members. Accordingly, organizational leaders have always paid some degree of attention to identifying and implementing effective leadership styles and behaviors even when organizational activities and human resources have been limited to a single cultural setting. However, as globalization increases it becomes even more imperative for organizations to appreciate the need to identify and select leaders with the skills to oversee managers and employees operating in a diverse cultural environment including the ability to recognize that cultural differences do impact the effectiveness of leaders and the success of the strategies they choose to as the means for leading. Various suggestions have been made regarding the competencies that leaders need to develop in order to be effective in overseeing organizations that include a multiplicity of diverse cultures. For example, a suggested list of important cross-cultural competencies for global leaders might include the following[53]:

- Leaders need to understand business, political, and cultural environments worldwide.
- Leaders need to learn the perspectives, tastes, trends, and technologies of many other cultures.
- Leaders need to be able to work simultaneously with people from many cultures.
- Leaders must be able to adapt to living and communicating in other cultures.

---

[53] See Adler, N.J., and S. Bartholomew. 1992. "Managing Globally Competent People." *Academy of Management Executive* 6, no. 3, pp. 52–65, 53; and Ting-Toomey, S. 1999. *Communicating Across Cultures*. New York, NY: Guilford; See also Kumar, R., B. Anjum, and A. Sinha. 2011. "Cross-Cultural Interactions and Leadership Behaviour." *International Refereed Research Journal* 2, no. 3, p. 151; Caligiuri, P., and I. Tarique. October 2012. "Dynamic Cross-Cultural Competencies and Global Leadership Effectiveness." Journal of World Business 47, no. 4, p. 612; and Hewlett, S. October 13, 2016. "The Attributes of an Effective Global Leader." *Harvard Business Review*.

- Leaders must learn how to relate to people from other cultures from a position of equality rather than cultural superiority.
- Leaders must be able to create a transcultural vision for the direction of the organization and develop and use communication skills that will allow them to articulate and implement that vision in a diverse workplace.

Dickson et al. wrote that "cross-cultural leaders," like cross-cultural researchers, must be open to differences they encounter when interacting with other cultures, show respect for cultures and cultural values that are different from their own, be able to understand and overcome their own acculturation, and recognize what aspects of their own value systems are a product of their own cultural experience.[54] Another relevant article included a definition of a "transcultural creative leader" as someone who is able to learn how to "(1) transcend their childhood acculturation and respect very different cultures; (2) build cross-cultural partnerships of mutual trust, respect, and obligation; (3) engage in cross-cultural creative problem solving to resolve conflicts; and (4) help construct third cultures in various operations."[55]

The information from the Global Leadership and Organizational Effectiveness ("GLOBE") project and similar studies can assist leaders in a number of ways.[56] For example, leaders reviewing the findings can gain a better understanding of their own culturally based biases and preferences and the fact that persons from other societal cultures may have different

---

[54] Dickson, M.W., D.N. Den Hartog, and J.K. Mitchelson. 2003. "Research on Leadership in a Cross-Cultural Context: Making Progress, and Raising New Questions." *The Leadership Quarterly* 14, no. 6, pp. 729–68, 758 (citing Graen, G.B., C. Hui, M. Wakabayashi, and Z.M. Wang. 1997. "Cross-Cultural Research Alliances in Organizational Research." In *New Perspectives on International Industrial/Organizational Psychology*, eds. P. Earley and M. Erez, 160–89. San Francisco, CA: Jossey-Bass.)

[55] Graen, G., and C. Hui. 1999. "Transcultural Global Leadership in the Twenty-First Century: Challenges and Implications for Development." In *Advances in Global Leadership*, ed. W. Mobley, 19–26, 1 Vols. Stamford, CT: JAI Press.

[56] The discussion in this section is derived from Northouse, P. 2006. *Leadership: Theory and Practice*, 326, 4th ed. Thousand Oaks, CA: Sage.

preferences and expectations regarding leadership behaviors. One area of concern is "ethnocentrism," which has been described as the tendency for individuals (e.g., leaders) to place their own group (ethnic, racial, or cultural) at the center of their observations of others and the world.[57] Although it is natural for people to give priority and value to their own beliefs, attitudes, and values over those of other groups, ethnocentrism endangers a cross-cultural leader's ability to act effectively if he or she perceives that his or her culture is "better" than the culture of others and thus is unwilling or unable to recognize the unique perspectives of people from different cultures. For example, a U.S. manager who endorses the concept of individual achievement that is strongly embedded in U.S. cultural values may have difficulty leading employees from societies that prefer collectivity—group members working closely together to achieve shared goals—unless the leader is able and willing to recognize and respect the beliefs and values that prevail in the other societal culture. This does not mean that the leader should abandon all of his or her culturally based beliefs and values; however, the leader must be mindful of any tendency toward ethnocentrism and be able to anticipate in advance what the reaction might be to certain decisions, policies, or modes of communication in other cultural contexts.

A concept, and another potential danger for effective leadership, which is related to ethnocentrism is "prejudice," which has been aptly defined as a largely fixed attitude, belief, or emotion held by an individual about another individual or group that is based on faulty or unsubstantiated data.[58] Racial prejudice is a well-known phenomenon in the United States and other countries; however, other types of prejudices can and do impact relations between leaders and followers and among members of groups and organizations including sexism, ageism, and homophobia. In general, everyone holds some degree of prejudice, and prejudices can be difficult to overcome given that "enlightenment" requires investment of time and effort to repair the faulty data upon which the prejudice is based and often going against the predominant attitudes and beliefs of others in a community or organizational context. However, effective

---

[57] Id. at p. 303.
[58] Id. at p. 304.

leaders simply cannot afford to let prejudices impede their judgment or poison the environment in which their followers must operate and collaborate and progressive organizations have launched substantial efforts to reduce and eradicate prejudice and cultural misunderstanding among their members. As previously noted, an effective cross-cultural leader is someone who shows respect for different cultures and cultural values and who has transcended childhood acculturation.

In addition, the information about how other societies perceive leadership can be used by leaders to adapt their styles and behaviors in order to be more effective when working with subordinates with different cultural backgrounds. A specific application would be learning new communication methods that can be used to convey ideas and directions, and gather information, more effectively in different cultural contexts. Information is part of the broader process of directly experiencing different cultures in order to understand how they work and reduce the anxiety that accompanies interactions with thoughts and behaviors that are "new." The more that a leader knows about the cultural attitudes of his or her followers the less likely they are to succumb to stereotyping and they can begin to identify and practice culturally appropriate leadership behaviors and communications skills. Successful cross-cultural communications require attention to a number of details including customs regarding opening and closing conversions, taking turns during conversations and interruptions, the use of silence and humor, and knowing when to close off a presentation of opinion or debate on a particular topic.[59]

Finally, the findings from the GLOBE project and other cross-cultural studies can be used by leaders and their organizations to improve the design of employee training programs, increase the effectiveness of global business teams, and facilitate integration of human resources acquired in

---

[59] Derived from Schuler, A.J., and D. Psy. 2018. "Tips for Successful Cross Cultural Communication." http://schulersolutions.com/cross_cultural_communication.html (accessed December 10, 2018). As a condition of use of his writings, Dr. Schuler requires the following notice: "Dr. A.J. Schuler is an expert in leadership and organizational change. To find out more about his programs and services, visit www.SchulerSolutions.com or call (703) 370-6545."

cross-border mergers and acquisitions activities.[60] These are all key issues for expanding businesses given the significant investment that firms make in sending home country managers and employees to foreign countries and supporting the activities of foreign subsidiaries. It is essential for the leaders of global organizations to provide their managers and employees with the tools necessary to collaborative efficiently and productively with colleagues spread around the world. For example, a strong global business team can facilitate customization of products to suit local requirements and promote transfer of new ideas and technologies from centers of excellence outside of the home country of the organization.

The advice to leaders hoping to be successful in identifying and coping with cultural diversity has been simply put by Bhawuk and Brislin:

> To be effective in another culture, people must be interested in
> other cultures, be sensitive enough to notice cultural differences,
> and then also be willing to modify their behavior as an indication
> of respect for the people of other cultures.[61]

Bennett and his colleagues created the "developmental model of intercultural sensitivity" as a guide to the steps that people can be expected to go through from the time that they are confronted with cultural differences to the point where they can incorporate an understanding of those differences into the way that they think and act so as to be able to interact effectively and cooperatively with people from different cultural backgrounds.[62] They suggested six stages, the first three being more

---

[60] Bing, J.W. 2004. "Hofstede's Consequences: The Impact of his Work on Consulting and Business Practices." *Academy of Management Executive* 18, no. 1, pp. 80–87.

[61] Bhawuk, D., and R. Brislin. 1992. "The Measurement of Intercultural Sensitivity using the Concepts of Individualism and Collectivism." *International Journal of Intercultural Relations* 16, no. 4, pp. 413–36, 416.

[62] The summary in this paragraph is adapted from Connerley, M.L., and P.B. Pedersen. 2005. *Leadership in a Diverse and Multicultural Environment: Developing Awareness, Knowledge, and Skills*, 47–49. Thousand Oaks, CA: Sage Publications, For further discussion, see, e.g., Bennett, M.J. 1993. "Towards Ethnorelativism: A Developmental Model of Intercultural Sensitivity." In *Education for the*

"ethnocentric" (i.e., the person's own culture is experienced as central to his or her reality) and the second three being more ethnorelative (i.e., the person's own culture is experienced in the context of other cultures). The ethnocentric stages include denial of differences—the person's own culture is experienced as the only reality; defense against differences (reversal)—other cultures are recognized yet viewed negatively and the person's own culture is perceived as being the only one that is "viable"; and minimization of differences—superficial cultural differences are accepted but other cultures are not yet accepted as viable alternatives. The ethnorelative stages include acceptance of differences—the person finally acknowledges that his or her own culture is experienced as just one of several viable alternatives; adaptation to differences—using newly developed communication skills a person begins to frame his or her reference to understand other cultures and be understood by persons from other cultures; and integration of differences—internalization of bicultural or multicultural frames of reference.

Intercultural Experience, ed. R. Paige, 21–71. Yarmouth, ME: Intercultural Press; Hammer, M.R., M.J. Bennett, and R. Wiseman. 2003. "Measuring Intercultural Sensitivity: The Intercultural Development Inventory." *International Journal of Intercultural Relations* 27, no. 4, pp. 421–43.

CHAPTER 3

Leadership Traits and Attributes

Introduction

There is no doubt that extensive resources have been devoted to the search for "traits" and "attributes" of effective leaders, as well as characteristics of dysfunctional leaders. In fact, one of the earliest and most popular conceptions of leadership that flourished in the 19th and early 20th centuries, often referred to as the "great man" theory, assumed that certain individual characteristics, or "traits," could be found in leaders but not in nonleaders and that those characteristics could not be developed but must be inherited.[1] Much of the work based on this theory was conducted under the umbrella of settling debates about whether leaders were "born or made" and, to the extent that genes were not totally responsible for leadership success, what strategies could be used to teach people how to execute the behaviors thought to be associated with effective leadership.

Eventually the "great man" theory was discredited in the face of a continuous stream of new theories that had as one of their core principles the democratization of leadership opportunities. However, the "great man" theory did leave behind a keen interest in attempting to identify those individual traits that could be most tightly linked to leadership and laid the foundation for the "trait school of leadership," which held that the traits of leaders—assumed to include their capacities, motives, and

---

[1] Kirkpatrick, S., and E. Locke. 1991. "Leadership: Do Traits Matter?" *Academy of Management Executive* 5, no. 2, pp. 48–60, 48. For an interesting exploration of the "great man" theory, including exhaustive citations, see Eckmann, H. 2018. "Great Man Theory: A Personal Account of Attraction." *Paper for the IBA Conference*, http://jameslconsulting.com/documents/GreatManTheory.pdf (accessed December 14, 2018).

patterns of behavior—were different from those of nonleaders. In contrast to the "great man" theory, trait theories did not particularly care whether the leadership traits were inherited or acquired and, in fact, early suggestions about optimal traits included items that were inherited (e.g., height, weight, and physique) as well as items that were dependent on experience and training (e.g., industry knowledge).[2]

Two of the most significant reviews of the trait school of leadership are attributed to Stodgill[3] and Mann[4] and there is evidence to support the proposition that certain traits, such as intelligence and dominance, are associated with leadership. However, many leadership scholars lacked confidence in the research findings relating to leadership traits. Muczyk and Adler noted that many of the traits associated with leaders appeared to have a genetic component and that this buoyed the arguments of those who maintained that leaders are "born"; however, they also argued that leadership success depended on the behaviors of those who sought to lead in particular situations and that, as such, the fact that most of these behaviors could be taught supported the view that leaders can also be "made." They conceded that leaders with certain genetic traits or natural gifts might be predisposed to various types of behaviors, and that this might make their job easier, but that the bottom line was the "traits are not the determining factor when it comes to leadership success."[5]

[2] Kirkpatrick, S., and E. Locke. 1991. "Leadership: Do Traits Matter?" *Academy of Management Executive* 5, no. 2, pp. 48–60, 48. Kirkpatrick and Locke suggested that further information on trait theories and particular traits could be obtained by a review of Stogdill, R. 1974. *Handbook of Leadership*. New York, NY: Free Press; Boyatzis, R. 1982. *The Competent Manager*. New York, NY: Wiley & Sons; Cox, C., and C. Cooper. 1988. *High Flyers: An Anatomy of Managerial Success*. Oxford: Basil Blackwell; and Yukl, G. 1989. *Leadership in Organizations*. Englewood Cliffs, NJ: Prentice Hall. Chapter 9.

[3] Stogdill, R.M. 1948. "Personal Factors Associated with Leadership: A Survey of the Literature." *Journal of Psychology* 25, pp. 35–71.

[4] Mann, R. 1959. "A Review of the Relationship Between Personality and Performance in Small Groups." *Psychological Bulletin* 56, pp. 241–70.

[5] Muczyk, J., and T. Adler. 2002. "An Attempt at a Consentience Regarding Formal Leadership." *Journal of Leadership and Organizational Studies* 9, no. 2, pp. 2–17.

Kirkpatrick and Locke acknowledged that trait theories were largely abandoned for a significant period of time; however, they noted that new research using a variety of methods had provided support for the general proposition that effective and successful leaders were "different" and that there were a handful of core traits that were extremely important contributors to, albeit not guarantors of, the success of leaders in the business world.[6] They cautioned, however, that "[t]raits alone ... are not sufficient for successful business leadership—they are only a precondition" and that aspiring leaders with those traits must take certain actions in order to be successful such as formulating a vision, role modeling, and setting goals.[7] There has clearly been a decline in the proportional interest in trait theories among published articles relating to leadership studies topics; however, even though "traits" alone do not tell the whole story behind effective leadership, it is nonetheless useful to survey some of the characteristics and attributes that have been frequently mentioned by researchers and other commentators.[8]

---

[6] Kirkpatrick, S., and E. Locke. 1991. "Leadership: Do Traits Matter?" *Academy of Management Executive* 5, no. 2, pp. 48–60, 49.

[7] Id.

[8] For detailed discussion of the research relating to personal attributes of leaders and "traits of leadership," see Bass, B.M., and R. Bass. 2009. *The Bass Handbook of Leadership: Theory, Research and Managerial Applications*. New York, NY: Simon and Schuster. Bass is well known for his model of "transformational leadership" and Tichy and Devanna identified a list of characteristics or traits of transformational leaders that included the following: identification of self as a change agent, courage, belief in people, value-driven, lifelong learner, able to deal with complexity, and "visionary". Tichy, N., and M. Devanna. 1986. *The Transformational Leader*. New York, NY: John Wiley & Sons. See also Craig, N., and S. Snook. May 2014. "From Purpose to Impact." *Harvard Business Review*; Patel, D. March 22, 2017. "11 Powerful Traits of Successful Leaders." *Forbes*. https://forbes.com/sites/deeppatel/2017/03/22/11-powerful-traits-of-successful-leaders/#3848103e469f; Gordon, J. 2017. *Power of Positive Leadership*. New York, NY: Wiley. (traits of positive leaders including positive culture, vision, optimism, confrontation and transformation of negativity, united and effective teams, purpose, grit, and pursuit of excellence); and Craig, N. 2018. *Leading from Purpose: Clarity and Confidence to Act When It Matters*. London: Nicholas Brealey Publishing.

Leadership Traits and Attributes

- **Self-Awareness**: Emotional self-awareness (i.e., ability to read and understand your emotions and recognize their impact on work performance and relationships); accurate self-assessment (i.e., a realistic evaluation of your strengths and limitations); and self-confidence (i.e., a strong and positive sense of self-worth and ability to demonstrate authentic "grace under pressure")
- **Self-Management**: Self-control (i.e., ability to keep disruptive emotions and impulses under control); credibility; trustworthiness (i.e., consistent display of honesty and integrity and excellent reputation); conscientiousness (i.e., ability to manage yourself and your responsibilities); and adaptability (i.e., skill at adjusting to changing situations and overcoming obstacles)
- **Drive**: Achievement orientation (i.e., drive to meet an internal standard of excellence); initiative (i.e., a readiness to seize opportunities); ambition regarding work and career leading to establishment of hard, challenging goals for themselves and their organizations; high levels of energy and stamina; and tenacity and persistence
- **Leadership Motivation and Effective Use of Power**: Strong desire to influence and lead others and willingness to assume responsibility; willingness to exercise his or her power over subordinates, issue directions to subordinates, and make appropriate use of positive and negative sanctions; ability to use power intelligently to achieve desired goals, or a vision (i.e., development of networks and coalitions, resolution of conflicts in a constructive manner, and effective use of role modeling in influencing others)
- **Social Awareness**: Empathy (i.e., skill at sensing other people's emotions, understanding their perspective, and taking an active interest in their work and concerns); organizational awareness (i.e., ability to read the currents of organizational life, build decision networks, and navigate politics); selective demonstration of weaknesses

and vulnerability to reveal approachability and humanity; and service orientation (i.e., ability to recognize and meet customers' needs)

- **Social Skill**: Visionary leadership (i.e., ability to take charge and inspire with a compelling vision); influence (i.e., ability to wield a range of persuasive tactics); developing others (i.e., propensity to bolster abilities of others through feedback and guidance); communication (i.e., skill at listening and at sending clear and convincing messages); change catalyst (i.e., proficiency in initiating new ideas and leading people in a new direction); conflict management (i.e., ability to de-escalate disagreements and orchestrate resolutions); building bonds (i.e., proficiency at cultivating and maintaining relationships); and teamwork and collaboration (i.e., competence at promoting cooperation and building teams).
- **Cognitive Ability**: Requisite level of relevant "cognitive ability" (i.e., strong analytical ability, good judgment, and capacity to think strategically and multidimensionally) to create a perception of competence in the minds of followers regarding the leader's ability to manage information intelligently and use it to effectively identify problems, formulate strategies and solutions, and make informed decisions
- **Knowledge of Business**: High degree of task-related knowledge about the company, industry, and technical matters; networking and cognitive ability to collect and understand information central to the organization and its business and necessary for understanding concerns of subordinates and making intelligent decisions; and sufficient demonstrable expertise regarding business to engage in behaviors that provide "leadership by example"

Goleman

In his well-known article on "What Makes a Leader?," Goleman argued that "effective leaders are alike in one crucial way: they all have a high degree of 'emotional intelligence.'"[9] Goleman described "emotional intelligence" as "the ability to manage ourselves and our relationships effectively."[10] In Goleman's first model, the "emotional intelligence" of a leader operating in the workplace context consisted of five fundamental capabilities, each of which had its own specific set of competencies and traits[11]:

1. Self-awareness, defined as the leader's ability to recognize and understand his or her moods, emotions, and drives, as well as their effect on others. Hallmarks of this trait include self-confidence, realistic self-assessment, and self-deprecating sense of humor.

2. Self-regulation, defined as the leader's ability to control or redirect disruptive impulses and moods and the propensity of the leader to be able to suspend judgment and "think before acting." Hallmarks of this trait include trustworthiness and integrity, comfort with ambiguity, and openness to change.

3. Motivation, defined as a passion to work for reasons that go beyond money or status and a propensity to pursue goals with energy and persistence. Hallmarks of this trait include a strong drive to achieve; optimism, even in the face of failure; and organizational commitment.

4. Empathy, defined as the leader's ability to understand the emotional makeup of other people and the ability of the leader to treat people according to their emotional reactions. Hallmarks of this trait include expertise in building and retaining talent, cross-cultural sensitivity, and service to clients and customers.

5. Social skill, defined as proficiency in managing relationships and building networks and the ability to find common ground and build rapport. Hallmarks of this trait include effectiveness in leading change, persuasiveness, and expertise in building and leading teams.

---

[9] Goleman, D. November–December 1998. "What Makes a Leader?" *Harvard Business Review* 76, no. 6, pp. 93–102. See also http://danielgoleman.info/emotional-intelligence-and-leadership/

[10] Goleman, D. March–April 2000. "Leadership That Gets Results." *Harvard Business Review*, pp. 78–90.

[11] Id.

Several years later, Goleman modified his model slightly by reducing the number of "capabilities" from five to four—"motivation" was removed and subsumed into "social skill"—and changing the names of two other capabilities to arrive at the following[12]:

1. Self-Awareness: Emotional self-awareness (i.e., the ability to read and understand your emotions, as well as recognize their impact on work performance, relationships, and the like); accurate self-assessment (i.e., a realistic evaluation of your strengths and limitations); and self-confidence (i.e., a strong and positive sense of self-worth).

2. Self-Management: Self-control (i.e., the ability to keep disruptive emotions and impulses under control); trustworthiness (i.e., a consistent display of honesty and integrity); conscientiousness (i.e., the ability to manage yourself and your responsibilities); adaptability (i.e., skill at adjusting to changing situations and overcoming obstacles); achievement orientation (i.e., the drive to meet an internal standard of excellence); and initiative (i.e., a readiness to seize opportunities).

3. Social Awareness: Empathy (i.e., skill at sensing other people's emotions, understanding their perspective, and taking an active interest in their concerns); organizational awareness (i.e., the ability to read the currents of organizational life, build decision networks, and navigate politics); and service orientation (i.e., the ability to recognize and meet customers' needs).

4. Social Skill: Visionary leadership (i.e., the ability to take charge and inspire with a compelling vision); influence (i.e., the ability to wield a range of persuasive tactics); developing others (i.e., the propensity to bolster the abilities of others through feedback and guidance); communication (i.e., skill at listening and at sending clear, convincing, and well-tuned messages); change catalyst (i.e., proficiency in initiating new ideas and leading people in a new direction); conflict management (i.e., the ability to de-escalate disagreements and orchestrate resolutions); building bonds (i.e., proficiency at cultivating and maintaining a web of relationships); and teamwork and collaboration (i.e., competence at promoting cooperation and building teams).

---

[12] Goleman, D. November–December 1998. "What Makes a Leader?" *Harvard Business Review* 76, no. 6, pp. 93–102.

Goleman noted that leaders do need other traits, such as general intelligence ("IQ") and technical skills; however, he believed that these were "threshold capabilities" or "entry-level requirements for executive positions" and that his research, along with the work of others, confirmed that emotional intelligence was the "sine qua non of leadership" and that without it a person could not become a "great leader" even though the person may have the best training, an incisive and analytical mind, and an endless supply of smart ideas.[13] On the surface, it would appear that Goleman cast his vote with those researchers in the "leaders are born not made" group who insist that there are certain traits that one either has or does not have, in this case emotional intelligence. However, whereas Goleman conceded there is a genetic component to many of the traits that he associated with emotional intelligence, he pointed out that research and practice indicated that emotional intelligence can be learned, although admittedly it will take a lot of hard work to train and discipline executives to become more empathetic and regulate their predisposition to act before thinking.

Goffee and Jones

In their theory about the "four essential qualities of leadership," Goffee and Jones identified the following traits and behaviors associated with inspirational leaders[14]:

1. They selectively show their weaknesses and, by exposing some vulnerability, they also reveal their approachability and humanity.

---

[13] Id. See also Goleman, D. 1995. *Emotional Intelligence.* New York, NY: Bantam; Goleman, D. 1998. *Working with Emotional Intelligence.* New York, NY: Bantam; and Goleman, D. March–April 2000. "Leadership That Gets Results." *Harvard Business Review* 78, no. 2, pp. 78–90, 80. (citing findings by McClelland "that leaders with strengths in a critical mass of six or more emotional intelligence competencies were far more effective than peers who lacked such strengths" based on various measures such as financial performance of their organizations, annual bonuses, and performance review assessments).

[14] Goffee, R., and G. Jones. September–October 2000. "Why Should Anyone Be Led by You?" *Harvard Business Review*, pp. 63–70.

2. They rely heavily on intuition to gauge the appropriate timing and course of their actions, and their ability to collect and interpret "soft data" helps them in knowing just when and how to take action.

3. They manage employees with "tough empathy," which means that they are able to empathize passionately—and realistically—with people and they care deeply about the work being carried out by their employees.

4. They reveal their differences and capitalize on their unique traits and skills.

Goffee and Jones conceded that there are leaders without these qualities that have been able to deliver superior financial returns; however, they believed that these qualities were essential to inspiring and motivating people, a state of affairs which certainly makes it easier for the leader to drive an organization toward success provided that he or she is also able to select and articulate the right direction. It is also worth noting the Goffee and Jones identified what they considered to be several "myths about leadership" and reported that based on their research it was not true that everyone can be a leader, leaders did not always deliver business results, people who get to the top of the organizational hierarchy are not necessarily leaders, and leaders are rarely great coaches.[15]

Kirkpatrick and Locke

After acknowledging that "trait" theories had fallen out of favor during the middle of the 20th century, Kirkpatrick and Locke argued that recent research had provided evidence to support the general proposition that certain traits do matter and significantly contributed to the success of business leaders and distinguished them from others.[16] According to Kirkpatrick and Locke, there are six traits on which leaders differ from

---

[15] Id. See also Goffee, R., and G. Jones. 2019. Why Should Anyone Be Led by You? With a New Preface by the Authors: What It Takes to Be an Authentic Leader. Cambridge MA: Harvard Business Review Press.

[16] Kirkpatrick, S., and E. Locke. 1991. "Leadership: Do Traits Matter?" *Academy of Management Executive* 5, no. 2, pp. 48–60.

nonleaders: drive, the desire to lead, honesty/integrity, self-confidence, cognitive ability, and knowledge of the business. Other traits, specifically charisma, creativity/originality, and flexibility, may also be important for leadership in certain instances; however, Kirkpatrick and Locke observed that the evidence regarding these traits was less clear-cut.[17] They acknowledged that other traits might be needed for effective leadership but elected to focus on the six "core" traits described in more detail in the following sections.

Drive

Kirkpatrick and Locke used the term drive "to refer to a constellation of traits and motives reflecting a high effort level."[18] In particular, they focused on five particular elements which they referred to as achievement motivation, ambition, energy, tenacity, and initiative:

1. *Achievement*: Kirkpatrick and Locke observed that leaders "have a relatively high desire for achievement" and that high achievers "obtain satisfaction from successfully completing challenging tasks, attaining standards of excellence, and developing better ways of doing things."[19] Persons aspiring for leadership status have a desire to complete challenging tasks and assignment as they progress in order to increase their technical expertise and initiate and execute organizational changes.

2. *Ambition*: According to Kirkpatrick and Locke, "[l]eaders are very ambitious about their work and careers and have a desire to get ahead."[20] Studies have indicated that effective leaders are more

---

[17] Id. at p. 56. Kirkpatrick and Locke did note, however, that "[f]lexibility or adaptiveness may be important traits for a leader in today's turbulent environment."

[18] Id. at p. 49. For evidence and further information regarding "drive," see Bass, B.M. 1990. *Handbook of Leadership*. New York, NY: The Free Press; Smith, K., and J. Harrison. 1986. "In Search of Excellent Leaders." In *Handbook of Strategy*, eds. W. Guth. New York, NY: Warren, Gorham, & Lamont.

[19] Id. at p. 49.

[20] Id. at p. 50. One study of managers at AT&T found ambition—the desire for advancement—was the strongest indicator of success 20 years later. See

ambitious than nonleaders and, in order for them to advance, persons seeking leadership positions look for opportunities to demonstrate their drive and determination. Kirkpatrick and Locke also noted that high ambition causes leaders to "set hard, challenging goals for themselves and their organizations."[21]

3. *Energy*: Leaders have the physical, mental, and emotional vitality to maintain a steadily productive work pace and put in the long and intense periods of time, extending for decades, required in order to fulfill their drive for achievement. Kirkpatrick and Locke noted that "leaders are more likely than nonleaders to have a high level of energy and stamina and to be generally active, lively, and often restless."[22]

4. *Tenacity*: Kirkpatrick and Locke observed that "[l]eaders are better at overcoming obstacles than nonleaders" and have a "degree of strength of will or perseverance."[23] This is important because the types of projects that leaders take on, such as organizational change programs, typically take a long time to execute and provide benefits and must frequently overcome strong institutional resistance. As such, leaders must be tirelessly persistent in championing these projects and relentless in their efforts to make sure that the desired changes take hold within the organization.[24]

5. *Initiative*: Kirkpatrick and Locke argued that effective leaders are "proactive" and that they make choices and initiate actions to create change rather than simply reacting to events or waiting for events to happen. Leaders are not willing to sit idly by and hope that good things will happen to them and prefer instead to take their own initiative to challenge the process.[25]

Howard, A., and D. Bray. 1988. *Managerial Lives in Transition: Advancing Age and Changing Times*. New York, NY: Guilford Press.

[21] Id. at p. 50.

[22] Id.

[23] Id. at p. 51.

[24] Kirkpatrick and Locke noted, however, that persistence is only a positive trait if used intelligently and that "[d]ogged pursuit of an inappropriate strategy can ruin an organization." Id.

[25] Id. at pp. 51–52.

Leadership Motivation and Effective
Use of Power

Kirkpatrick and Locke noted that whereas the various characteristics associated with "drive" are admirable they may sometimes cause a prospective leader to believe that he or she must do everything on his or her own, a situation that can lead to problems with development commitment and responsibility among subordinates. It is therefore important, in the opinion of Kirkpatrick and Locke, that leaders supplement their own drive and ambition with a true desire to lead others, a characteristic referred to as "leadership motivation."[26] Kirkpatrick and Locke cited research findings that indicate that effective leaders have a strong desire to influence and lead others, prefer to be in a leadership rather than a subordinate role, and have a willingness to assume responsibility.[27]

Leadership motivation is often associated with the "need for power" and it is commonly recognized that "power is a leader's currency, or the primary means through which the leader gets things done in the organization."[28] Assuming this to be true, it is understandable that prospective leaders strive to gain the power necessary to exercise influence over others in the organization, and Kirkpatrick and Locke emphasize that in order to be successful a leader must be willing to exercise his or her power over subordinates, issue directions to subordinates, and make appropriate use of positive and negative sanctions. However, according to McClelland, the effective use of that power depends on whether the leader has a "personalized" or "socialized" power motive. A leader with personalized power motive, sometimes described as "power lust," pursues power as an end in

---

[26] For evidence and further information regarding "leadership motivation," see Bentz, V. 1967. "The Sears Experience in the Investigation, Description, and Prediction of Executive Behavior." In *Measuring Executive Effectiveness*, eds. F. Wickert and D. McFarland. New York, NY: Appleton-Century-Crofts; and Miner, J. 1978. "Twenty Years of Research on Role-Motivation Theory of Managerial Effectiveness." *Personnel Psychology* 31, pp. 739–60.

[27] Kirkpatrick, S., and E. Locke. 1991. "Leadership: Do Traits Matter?" *Academy of Management Executive* 5, no. 2, pp. 48–60, 52.

[28] Id. (citing Bennis, W., and B. Nanus. 1985. *Leaders: The Strategies for Taking Charge*. New York, NY: Harper & Row.)

itself and exercises that power in ways that seek to dominate subordinates and make them submissive and dependent. In contrast, a leader with a socialized power motive uses power intelligently to achieve desired goals, or a vision, and "its use is expressed as the ability to develop networks and coalitions, gain cooperation from others, resolve conflicts in a constructive manner, and use role modeling in influencing others."[29]

Honesty/Integrity

Kirkpatrick and Locke conceded that honesty and integrity are important virtues for every person; however, they noted that in the area of leadership these factors are essential for effectiveness. They explained that "[i]ntegrity is the correspondence between word and deed and honesty refers to being truthful or non-deceitful" and that honesty and integrity are "the foundation of a trusting relationship between leader and followers."[30] Practices of successful leaders that demonstrate the requisite level of honesty and integrity include being open with their followers, yet discrete in not violating confidences or carefully disclosing harmful information. Kirkpatrick and Locke concluded that "[e]ffective leaders are credible, with excellent reputations, and high levels of integrity."[31]

Kouzes and Posner agreed:

> Honesty is absolutely essential to leadership. After all, if we are willing to follow someone, whether it be into battle or into the boardroom, we first want to assure ourselves that the person is worthy of our trust. We want to know that he or she is being truthful, ethical and principled. We want to be fully confident in the integrity of our leaders.[32]

---

[29] Id. at p. 53. For further discussion of McClelland's distinction between personalized and socialized power motives, see McClelland, D. 1965. "N-achievement and Entrepreneurship: A Longitudinal Study." *Journal of Personality and Social Psychology* 1, pp. 389–92.

[30] Id. at p. 53.

[31] Id. at p. 54.

[32] Kouzes, J., and B. Posner. 1989. *The Leadership Challenge: How to Get Things Done in Organizations.* San Francisco: Jossey-Bass. For evidence and further

In the same vein, a study undertaken by the Hay Group concluded that the most reliable predictor of employee satisfaction was trust and confidence in the top leadership of the organization and that achieving the desired organizational trust and confidence required that leaders effectively communicate with employees to help them understand the organization's overall business strategy and how they contributed to the achievement of the organization's key business objectives and share information with employees about the performance of the organization as a whole and each employee's business unit (i.e., division or department) in particular.[33]

Self-Confidence

Kirkpatrick and Locke argued that a leader's self-confidence, including others' perception of it, is important to his or her effectiveness as a leader for a number of reasons.[34] For example, self-confidence is crucial in making the decisions required of leaders and in gaining and holding the trust of those who will be called upon to carry out those decisions. Self-confidence is also needed to navigate the challenges of the often chaotic environment confronting the leader, including the need to gather and analyze large amounts of information, solve problems and make decisions under tight time constraints, balance and reconcile competing interests, overcome setbacks, manage risks and uncertainties, and cope with unforeseen events. In addition, Kirkpatrick and Locke noted that self-confidence is generally related to emotional stability and that confident leaders are better able to remain even-tempered while confronting the challenges of their position and resolving conflicts and representing the organiza-

---

information regarding "honesty" and "integrity," see Bass, B.M. 1990. *Handbook of Leadership*. New York: The Free Press; Bennis, W., and B. Nanus. 1985. *Leaders: The Strategies for Taking Charge*. New York, NY: Harper & Row; Peters, T. 1987. *Thriving on Chaos*. New York, NY: Harper & Row; and Rand, A. 1961. *For the New Intellectual: The Philosophy of Ayn Rand*. New York, NY: Signet.

[33] Lamb, L., and K. McKee. 2004. Applied Public Relations: Cases in Stakeholder Management. Mahwah, NJ: Lawrence Erlbaum Associates/Routledge.

[34] Kirkpatrick, S., and E. Locke. 1991. "Leadership: Do Traits Matter?" *Academy of Management Executive* 5, no. 2, pp. 48–60, 54.

tion in interactions with outsiders. Kirkpatrick and Locke referenced an article that highlighted the notion that effective leaders demonstrate "grace under pressure" that calms their followers.[35] Finally, self-confidence allows leaders to see challenges and chaotic events as opportunities for development and situations where they can indeed make a difference.[36]

Cognitive Ability

A number of researchers have emphasized the significant demands on leaders with respect to collecting, organizing, and analyzing large amounts of information from disparate sources. These challenges have been exacerbated by advances in information technology that have enabled a virtual avalanche of data and communications that often seem overwhelming. It is not surprising therefore that Kirkpatrick and Locke suggested that leaders must have the requisite level of "cognitive ability" to manage information intelligently and use it to effectively identify problems, formulate strategies and solutions, and, in general, make informed decisions about issues relating to their organizations.[37] Having the requisite "cognitive ability" does not necessarily mean that a leader must be "brilliant"; however, Kirkpatrick and Locke cited Kotter for the view that effective

---

[35] Id. at p. 55 (citing Labich, K. October 24, 1988. "The Seven Keys to Business Leadership." *Fortune*, pp. 58–66).

[36] For evidence and further information regarding "self-confidence," see Bass, B.M. 1990. *Handbook of Leadership*. New York, NY: The Free Press; Bennis, W., and B. Nanus. 1985. *Leaders: The Strategies for Taking Charge*. New York, NY: Harper & Row; Maddi, S., and S. Kobasa. 1984. *The Hardy Executive: Health Under Stress*. Chicago: Dorsey Professional Books; and McCall, M, Jr., and M. Lombardo. 1983. *Off the Track: Why and How Successful Executives get Derailed*. Technical Report No. 21, Greensboro, NC: Center for Creative Leadership.

[37] Kirkpatrick, S., and E. Locke. 1991. "Leadership: Do Traits Matter?" *Academy of Management Executive* 5, no. 2, pp. 48–60, 55. For evidence and further information regarding "cognitive ability," see Lord, R., C. DeVader, and G. Aliger. 1986. "A Meta-analysis of the Relation Between Personality Traits and Leadership Perceptions: An Application of Validity Generalization Procedures." *Journal of Applied Psychology* 61, pp. 402–10; Howard, A., and D. Bray. 1988. *Managerial Lives in Transition: Advancing Age and Changing Times*. New York, NY: Guilford Press.

leadership requires a "'keen mind' (i.e., strong analytical ability, good judgment, and the capacity to think strategically and multidimensionally)."[38] In addition, it is important that followers actually believe that their leader is "more capable in *some* respects than they are."[39]

Knowledge of the Business

Somewhat related to "cognitive knowledge" is the observation by Kirkpatrick and Locke that effective leaders demonstrate a "high degree of knowledge about the company, industry and technical matters."[40] Effective leaders are privy to extensive information about their firms and the industry and overall economy in which they are operating and this specific information in invaluable to their ability to make intelligent decisions regarding strategy and operational matters. Another important benefit of relevant technical expertise is that it enables leaders to have a clear understanding of the concerns of their subordinates and gives them credibility when they are offering advice on potential solutions to technical issues that may arise within the firm. Kirkpatrick and Locke cited the findings of various researchers that effective leaders tended to have long careers in the industry in which their firms were operating and that formal education was not necessarily a requirement for effective leadership as long as the leader had the cognitive ability to collect and understand the information that was central to the business of his or her organization.

Knowledge of the business is a particular form of "expertise" that plays a big role in the so-called "power and influence" theories of leadership. These theories, the most well known of which was put forward by French and Raven, focus on how leaders use power and influence in creating their

---

[38] Id. at p. 55. See Kotter, J. 1988. *The Leadership Factor*. New York, NY: Free Press.

[39] Id. at p. 55.

[40] Id. at p. 55. For evidence and further information regarding "knowledge of the business," see Bennis, W., and B. Nanus. 1985. *Leaders: The Strategies for Taking Charge*. New York, NY: Harper & Row; Kotter, J. 1986. *The General Managers*. New York, NY: Free Press; and Smith, K., and J. Harrison. 1986. "In Search of Excellent Leaders" In *Handbook of Strategy*, eds. W. Guth. New York, NY: Warren, Gorham, & Lamont.

leadership styles. French and Raven's "Five Forms of Power" included three forms of positional power—legitimate, reward, and coercive—and two forms of personal power referred to as expert and referent.[41] Proponents of this model have argued that personal power, particular expert, is the preferred alternative for leaders to be effective and influential on the basis of the perceptions of their followers that their leadership role is legitimate. The power of expertise can be enhanced by appropriate behaviors, such as "leading by example."

Management Implications

Kirkpatrick and Locke suggested several "management implications" from their findings regarding what they viewed as universally important "traits" of effective leaders.[42] First, they argued that cognitive ability is probably the least changeable or trainable of the six traits that they identified and that "drive" is fairly constant over time although they conceded that it could change. Second, both "drive" and the "desire to lead" really must be observed in order to be properly assessed and proper observation requires that employees in lower levels within the organization be given opportunities early in their careers to assume more responsibility and act with greater autonomy. Third, "knowledge of the business" and the accompanying technical knowledge can be acquired over a period of time through the proper balance of formal training and job experience complimented by a "thirst for knowledge" and desire to explore opportunities for learning. Prospective leaders and their companies can facilitate this process through job rotation programs. Fourth, task-specific self-confidence can be enhanced as business and technical knowledge is acquired and prospective leaders begin to learn and apply the skills that they will need in the future. Finally, with respect to "honesty," Kirkpatrick and Locke observe simply that "[h]onesty does not require skill building; it is a vir-

[41] For detailed discussion, see French, J., and B. Raven. 1959. "The Bases of Social Power." In *Group Dynamics*, eds. D. Cartwright and A. Zander. New York, NY: Harper & Row.

[42] Kirkpatrick, S., and E. Locke. 1991. "Leadership: Do Traits Matter?" *Academy of Management Executive* 5, no. 2, pp. 48–60, 58.

tue one achieves or rejects by choice" and that companies can promote the right choices through celebration of role models for honest behavior and refraining from rewarding, with compensation and/or promotions, dishonesty.

Muczyk and Adler

Muczyk and Adler themselves provided a lengthy list of leadership traits based on their review of the literature, including "passion to lead," "will to manage," a large reservoir of energy, organizing abilities, a mature personality, a requisite amount of intelligence, task-relevant knowledge, confidence, integrity, and adaptability.[43] They pointed out that high energy levels and adaptability are necessary for leaders to carry out many of the managerial roles described by Mintzberg and cope with change and the need to interact with a broad spectrum of stakeholders on behalf of their organizations. As for intelligence and task-relevant knowledge, they referred to the findings of Kirpatrick and Locke and noted that these traits were particularly useful in directing subordinates and answering their concerns and questions about specific job-related activities. Finally, they strongly endorsed the importance of integrity as part of the optimal leader profile as a prerequisite in securing the respect, trust, and goodwill of subordinates that is necessary in order to motivate to comply with the directions given by the leader.[44]

Principles and Attributes of Military Leadership

Not surprisingly, leadership has always been an important subject in military training and development programs and military leaders

---

[43] Muczyk, J., and T. Adler. 2002. "An Attempt at a Consentience Regarding Formal Leadership." *Journal of Leadership and Organizational Studies* 9, no. 2, pp. 2–17.

[44] Id. They referred to integrity, as well as the leader's willingness and ability to treat subordinates with "courtesy, dignity and respect," as integral parts of the "moral dimension of leadership". See also Muczyk, J., and T. Adler. 2014. "A Strategy for Climbing The Organizational Ladder." *Academy of Strategic Management Journal* 13, no. 2, p. 37.

are quoted on lists compiled to illustrate various definitions and conceptions of leadership. For example, Montgomery defined leadership as "the capacity and the will to rally men and women to a common purpose and the character which inspires confidence." MacArthur observed:

A true leader has the confidence to stand alone, the courage to make tough decisions, and the compassion to listen to the needs of others. He does not set out to be a leader, but becomes one by the equality of his actions and the integrity of his intent.

Leadership quotes from Eisenhower have included "leadership is the art of getting someone else to do something you want done because he wants to do it," "the supreme quality of leadership is integrity," and "you don't lead by hitting people over the head—that's assault, not leadership."

The U.S. Army has a long history of leadership training activities and Clark, drawing on training materials developed and used by the army, offered the following list of key "principles of leadership:"

- Know yourself and seek self-improvement.
- Be technically proficient.
- Seek responsibility and take responsibility for your actions.
- Make sound and timely decisions.
- Set the example.
- Know your people and look out for their well-being.
- Keep your workers informed.
- Develop a sense of responsibility in your workers.
- Ensure that tasks are understood, supervised, and accomplished.
- Train as a team.
- Use the full capabilities of your organization.

Clark went on to argue that in order to effectively implement the principles of leadership, leaders needed to concentrate on specific attributes that were divided into groups referred to as "Be" (i.e., who leader was as evidenced by beliefs and character), "Know" (i.e., what the leader knew regarding relevant jobs and tasks and human nature), and "Do" (i.e., what the leader did while carrying out his or her duties such as providing direction to followers and motivating followers). Specific recommendations were as follows:

- BE a professional (e.g., be loyal to the organization and take personal responsibility).
- BE a professional with good character traits (e.g., honesty, competence, candor, commitment, integrity, and courage).
- KNOW the four factors of leadership: leader, followers, communication, and situation.
- KNOW yourself (i.e., know the strengths and weaknesses of your character, knowledge, and skills).
- KNOW human nature (i.e., understand human needs, emotions, and how people respond to stress).
- KNOW your job (i.e., be proficient, be able to lead by example, and be willing to provide training and coaching to followers).
- KNOW your organization (i.e., understand the organizational culture and structure, how to ask for help and access resources, and who the informal leaders are among the followers).
- DO provide direction (i.e., set get goals and plan, make decisions, and identify and resolve problems and conflicts).
- DO implement (i.e., communicate, coordinate, supervise, and evaluate).
- DO motivate (e.g., develop morale and a positive organizational climate, train, coach, and counsel).

Source: D. Clark, "Concepts of Leadership," Big Dog and Little Dog's Performance Juxtaposition (blog) http://nwlink.com/~donclark/leader/leadcon.html (accessed June 15, 2015) (citing U.S. Army, Military Leadership: Field Manual 22-100 (Washington, DC: U.S.

Government Printing Office 1983). Clark's website also includes both short and long versions of a useful leadership self-assessment survey. Quotations from military leaders selected from a list compiled and presented in K. Kruse, 365 Inspirational Quotes: Daily Motivation For Your Best Year Ever (Wholehearted Leadership Press 2014)).

Networking and Leadership Development

Hoppe and Reinelt suggested a framework for classifying networks with a particular focus on networks that organizational leaders might join as part of their leadership development efforts in order to gain access to resources and other support.[45] They noted that whereas leadership networks may be intentionally created, they also often emerge from a strong need or desire of the members of the networks to become and remain connected. The four types of networks in their framework were as follows:

- *Peer Leadership Network*: A peer network is based on social ties among leaders who are connected with one another on the basis of the shared interests and commitments, shared work, or shared experiences. A peer network provides leaders with access to resources that they believe are trustworthy and can be used by leaders to share information, provide advice and support, learn from one another, and collaborate together. Gaining access to a peer network is often one of the fundamental goals of a leadership development program.
- *Organizational Leadership Network*: The social ties established in an organizational leadership network are focused on increasing performance. Ties in this type of network are often informal and exist outside of the formal organizational structure and provide leaders with the means to consult with colleagues outside of their departments or business units in order to solve problems more quickly. In some cases,

---

[45] Hoppe, B., and C. Reinelt. 2010. "Social Network Analysis and the Evolution of Leadership Networks." *The Leadership Quarterly* 21, p. 600, 601.

organizational networks are intentionally created, in the form
of cross-functional teams or communities of practice, to
bridge gaps in the formal organizational structure that may
be impeding performance and progress toward organizational
goals (e.g., completing a new product and/or delivering
services to customers more efficiently).

- *Field-Policy Leadership Network*: Leaders who share common
  interests and a commitment to influencing a field of practice
  or policy may come together to form a network that can
  be used to shape the environment surrounding the topic
  of mutual interest (e.g., frame the issue, clarify underlying
  assumptions, and/or establish standards for what is expected
  of key stakeholders). This type of network can be a powerful
  tool for collective advocacy on issues and policies that are
  of common importance to multiple organizations and can
  facilitate mobilization of support and allocation of resources.
- *Collective Leadership Network*: A collective leadership network,
  which is based on a common cause or share goals, emerges
  and enlarges over time. The process begins with local groupings that eventually interact with groups in other areas to
  form larger networks and a much broader community that
  allows members to pursue specific goals while feeling a part of
  something that is larger than oneself.

Hoppe and Reinelt emphasized that the framework was largely for
illustrative purposes and that many networks are actually hybrids of
multiple categories or simply fail to fit neatly into one of their network
types. What is important from a leadership development perspective
is the potential value of networks to current and prospective leaders in
terms of access to information, advice, support, and other learning benefits. Networking also provides leaders with a foundation for identifying potential collaborators for new initiatives and impacting the external
environment of the organizations they lead.

The relative position of leaders within their networks is an important consideration. In some cases, leaders enjoy strong ties to other members of their network ("bonding connections") and thus have a feeling of

affiliation and connectivity to a trusted community where interactions are familiar and efficient. However, leaders also need to have "bridging" or "brokerage" connections which, although weaker than bonding connections, nonetheless provide them with essential paths to accessing new resources and developing new opportunities for innovation and profit.[46] A "bridger" is a person in a network who has connections to different clusters and is typically someone who is deeply embedded in relaying information among other network members. In this capacity, a leader can gain recognition and trust as a key broker of access and knowledge and as someone who is positioned to move projects that require collaboration from people in different parts of the organizational network. As a leader's reputation grows, he or she is more likely to become a "hub" in a network, which means someone who is a highly sought resource for advice by other members of the network. The influence of a hub increases to the extent that the persons who seek his or her advice are themselves relatively more influential in the network.

---

[46] Id.

CHAPTER 4

Leadership Styles

Introduction

One of the most interesting, and voluminously researched, topics in leadership studies is "leadership style." In general, leadership style focuses on how leaders interact with their followers and has been more specifically defined as "the manner and approach of providing direction, motivating people and achieving objectives."[1] Whereas there are a number of different models of leadership style, several of which are discussed in the following sections, three fundamental dimensions are often represented: the leader's approach to influencing the behavior of his or her followers; the manner in which decisions regarding the direction of the group are made, with a specific emphasis on the level of participation offered to followers; and the balance struck between goal attainment and maintaining harmony within the group (sometimes referred to as group "maintenance").[2] For example, two alternative approaches to influencing the behavior of followers are the transactional leadership, which views the leader–follower relationship as a process of exchange, and transformational leadership, which relies on the leader's ability to communicate a clear and acceptable vision and related goals that engender intense emotion among followers that motivates them to buy into and pursue the leader's vision. Contrasting styles for decision-making are found when distinguishing authoritarian (autocratic) and participative (democratic) leaders. Finally, the balance between goals and maintenance is emphasized in those models, such as Blake and Mouton's Grid Theory, that analyze the degree to which

---

[1] Fertman, C.I., and J.A. van Liden. 1999. "Character Education: An Essential Ingredient for Youth Leadership Development." *NASSP Bulletin* 83, no. 609, pp. 9–15. See also Ashkenas, R., and B. Manville. 2018. *Harvard Business Review Leader's Handbook*. Cambridge MA: Harvard Business Press.

[2] Scholl, R. 2000. *What is Leadership Style?*

leaders exhibit task and/or relationship orientation in their interactions with followers.

Many commentators, notably Kotter, have observed that coping with change is one of the most important challenges confronting leaders of organizations, particularly given the unending pressures caused by globalization, innovations in technology and communications, and turbulent economic times.[3] Reardon et al. suggested that five phases of change could be identified—planning, enabling, launching, catalyzing, and maintaining—and that each required a leader to use one of four different types of leadership styles—commanding, logical, inspirational, or supportive—that was most appropriate for that phase.[4] Muczyk and Adler have questioned the feasibility of this model given that it calls for an uncommonly versatile and flexible leader.[5] However, other researchers who have studied the evolution of organizations have also concluded that appropriate leadership styles do tend to change as time goes by and that although it may not be feasible for a single leader to attempt to change his or her style, changes at the top of the organizational hierarchy may be needed from time to time in order to bring in the right person for the particular situation.[6]

---

[3] Kotter distinguished "leadership" from "management" and argued that it was the job of "leaders" to cope with change and set direction while managers tended to dealing with complexity and planning. See Kotter, J.P. March-April, 1995. "Leading Change: Why Transformation Efforts Fail." *Harvard Business Review OnPoint*, pp. 1–10; and Kotter, J. 1996. *Leading Change.* Cambridge, MA: Harvard Business School Press.

[4] Reardon, K.K., K.J. Reardon, and A.J. Rowe. 1998. "Leadership Styles for the Five Stages of Radical Change." *Acquisition Review Quarterly* 6, pp. 129–46.

[5] Muczyk, J., and T. Adler. 2002. "An Attempt at a Consentience Regarding Formal Leadership." *Journal of Leadership and Organizational Studies* 9, no. 2, pp. 2–17. Muczyk and Adler have also proposed the existence of a "leadership cycle" that anticipates a change in leadership style as organizations go through various stages of development.

[6] Id. (citing Muczyk, J., and B. Reimann. 1987. "The Case for Directive Leadership." *The Academy of Management Executive* 1, no. 3, pp. 301–11); Quinn, R., and K. Cameron. 1983. "Organizational Life Cycles and Some Shifting Criteria of Effectiveness: Some Preliminary Evidence." *Management Science* 29, no. 1,

Leadership Styles

Definitions and descriptions of leadership styles typically are based on three fundamental dimensions:

- The leader's approach to influencing the behavior of his or her followers
- The manner in which decisions regarding the direction of the group are made, with a specific emphasis on the level of participation offered to followers
- The balance struck between attaining goals and maintaining harmony within the group (sometimes referred to as group "maintenance")
- Among the styles included in representative models of leadership styles are the following:
- Authoritarian or autocratic; participative or democratic; and delegative or "free reign" (sometimes referred to as "laissez faire")
- Exploitive authoritative, benevolent authoritative, consultative system, and participative
- Country Club Leadership (High Concern for People/Low Concern for Production), Produce or Perish Leadership (Low Concern for People/High Concern for Production), Impoverished Leadership (Low Concern for People/Low Concern for Production), Middle-of-the-Road Leadership (Medium Concern for People/Medium Concern for Production), and Team Leadership (High Concern for People/ High Concern for Production)
- Directive autocrat, permissive autocrat, directive democrat, and permissive democrat

pp. 33–51; Greiner, L.E. July/August 1972. "Evolution and Revolution as Organizations Grow." *Harvard Business Review*, pp. 37–46; and Hersey, P., and K. Blanchard. 1988. *Management of Organizational Behavior*, 5th ed. Englewood Cliffs, N.J: Prentice-Hall.

- Coercive, authoritative, affiliative, democratic, pacesetting, and coaching
- Leadership "approaches": strategy, human assets, expertise, "box," and "change"
- Servant

Lewin's Three Styles of Leadership

The results of one of the earliest attempts to identify different styles of leadership using research methods were published by Lewin et al. in 1939. This study became quite influential in the field and led to the recognition of three major leadership styles, two of which became the foundation of further work by other researchers in the decades that followed: authoritarian or autocratic; participative or democratic; and delegative or "free reign" (sometimes referred to as "laissez faire").[7] Rather than conduct research in the context of a business organization, Lewin and his colleagues observed the behaviors of schoolchildren in response to different styles of leadership as they worked to complete an arts and crafts project. They concluded that good leaders use all three styles at some point in time; however, one style was usually the dominant style and democratic/participative leadership was generally the most effective approach. In contrast, poor leaders usually rely on one style regardless of the situation and are most likely to choose either the authoritarian/autocratic style or the delegate/laissez faire style.

Authoritarian or Autocratic Leadership

The authoritarian, or autocratic, leaders in Lewin et al.'s study provided members of their groups with clear expectations of what needed to be

---

[7] Lewin, K., R. Llippit, and R. White. 1939. "Patterns of Aggressive Behavior in Experimentally Created Social Climates." *Journal of Social Psychology* 10, no. 2, pp. 271–301. The summary of the results of the study by Lewin et al. in this section is derived from K. Cherry, "Lewin's Leadership Styles." http://psychology.about.com/od/leadership/a/leadstyles.htm (accessed December 14, 2018).

done and when and how the tasks and activities should be completed. All decisions were made by the leader without input from group members and there was a clear division between the leader and his or her followers. Not surprisingly, Lewin et al. found that the decisions made under the authoritarian style were less creative and that authoritarian leaders were often seen as being controlling, bossy, and dictatorial by their followers. In addition, authoritarian leaders had much more difficulty transitioning to a participative style than vice versa. All in all, authoritarian leadership was seen as being useful and efficient in limited circumstances, such as when there is little time for the group to participate in weighing options and making decisions and the leader is demonstrably more knowledgeable about the task at hand than the other members of the group.

Participative or Democratic Leadership

The distinguishing feature of participative, or democratic, leadership was the willingness of the leader to not only offer guidance to members of the group but also allow them to provide input into decisions regarding the objectives of the group and how those objectives should be pursued. There was less distance between the leader and his or her followers when the participative style was used and the leader was more involved in the routine interactions that typically occur in the group context. Although participative leaders retained the right to make the final decisions, group members felt more involved in the process and thus appeared to be more motivated and creative. Participative leaders were the most effective among the three styles studied by Lewin et al. Although members of the group were less productive than members of the autocratic group, Lewin et al. felt that the contributions of the members of the participative group were of higher quality than those who worked under an autocratic leader.

Delegative or Laissez Faire Leadership

Delegative, or laissez faire, leadership was the least effective of the three leadership styles and featured little or no guidance from the leaders to their followers. As a result, members of the group were forced to take on many of the roles typically carried out by the leader such as making decisions about the goals of the group and the best way to organize the work activities of group members. Lewin et al. found that the members of this group were unable to work independently, had trouble cooperating with one another, and made more demands on their leader. Although there may be situations where this type of style might work, such as when group members are highly qualified in a specific area of expertise, the general finding was that group members were poorly motivated and unproductive because of the lack of clearly defined objectives and roles. Whereas infrequently observed among U.S. managers, laissez-faire leadership behaviors do occur from time to time and, not surprisingly, research conducted after the study by Lewin et al. has indicated that this "style" of leadership generally has an adverse impact on work-related outcomes of followers.[8] Bass was also critical of laissez-faire leaders who avoided the proactive involvement associated with transformational and transactional leaders, a topic discussed elsewhere in this chapter, and who chose to "abdicate their responsibility and avoid making decisions," thus leaving their followers without guidance as to identifying and completing their job responsibilities.[9]

Likert's System Four model

Rensis Likert identified four systems of management that might be deployed within an organization.[10] The fundamental characteristic of

---

[8] Ardichvili, A., and K. Kuchinke. 2002. "Leadership Styles and Cultural Values Among Managers and Subordinates: A Comparative Study of Four Countries of the Former Soviet Union, Germany and the US." *Human Resource Development International* 5, no. 1, pp. 99–117, 102. (citing Bass, B.M., and R.M. Stogdill's. 1990. *Handbook of Leadership: Theory, Research & Managerial Applications*. New York, NY: The Free Press.) Yammarino, F.J., and B. Bass. 1990. "Long-term Forecasting of Transformational Leadership and its Effects Among Naval Officers: Some Preliminary Findings." In *Measures of Leadership*, 151–69, eds. K. Clark and M. Clark. Greensboro, NC: Center for Creative Leadership.

[9] Bass, B.M. 1990. "From Transactional to Transformational Leadership: Learning to Share the Vision." *Organizational Dynamics* 18, no. 3, pp. 19–31.

[10] Likert prepared and administered questionnaires to managers and employees in over 200 organizations that examined a number of key organizational

each of these systems was the dominant "style of leadership," which is the method that leaders within the organization used when determining the level of involvement of subordinates in decision-making and motivating subordinates to follow the directions issued by the leader. Likert categorized his four systems as follows:

1. The "exploitive authoritative" system is used by leaders that have low regard for subordinates (i.e., no trust or confidence) and are prepared to use threats and other fear-based methods to ensure that subordinates will comply with the decisions made by the leader. In this system subordinates are simply expected to follow the decisions made by their leaders without question or the opportunity to provide input. Communication channels when this system is used are downward and the social and psychological needs of subordinates are largely ignored. Completion of the work identified by the leaders is the only concern within the organization and there is no interest in encouraging or rewarding teamwork.

2. The "benevolent authoritative" system, sometimes referred to as "benevolent dictatorship," is still authoritarian (i.e., decisions are made solely by the leader); however, the leader does pay some attention to the concerns of subordinates and is willing to create a reward system to encourage subordinates to act in the manner directed by the leader as opposed to simply relying on threats and fear. Communication channels when this system is used are a bit more open although subordinates continue to be guarded about what they share with the leader and often limit their comments to what they think the leader wants to hear. The leader may delegate a small amount of authority, generally to a small group of managers who focus on making sure that those lower in the organizational hierarchy complete their tasks without straying from the directions provided from above, but all major decisions remain the sole province of the leader.

---

characteristics including leadership processes, motivational forces, communication processes, interaction-influence processes, decision-making processes, goal-setting or ordering procedures, and control processes. See Likert, R. 1967. *The Human Organization: Its Management and Value*, New York, NY: McGraw-Hill.

3. The "consultative" system features an authentic attempt by the leader to listen to the ideas and views of subordinates although the leader's explicit outreach to subordinates remains limited (but more active than if the benevolent authoritative system is used). Centralized decision-making remains the rule when this system is used; however, subordinates are motivated by rewards and some level of satisfaction that the leader is willing to hear and respect their opinions and their ideas for improving the way in which the organization operates. This system features more open horizontal and vertical communications than either of the authoritative systems although it is still the case that more information flows downward than upward.

4. The "participative" system features full use of participative methods by the leader to bring subordinates into the loop regarding major decisions and create an organizational culture in which the ideas of people at all levels are valued and people feel a psychological closeness and gain satisfaction from working closely together toward a shared goal. Leaders have a high level of confidence in the abilities of their subordinates and the work of the organization is conducted through teams that are linked by effective integrative strategies. Subordinates are committed to the goals of the organization and assume responsibility for achieving them because they are satisfied about the opportunities for meaningful participation in setting those goals and the leaders have designed a reward system that is closely aligned to those goals.

Based on his analysis of the responses to his questionnaires Likert concluded that organizational units that relied on either of the "authoritative" systems were the least productive and that units relying on either the consultative or participative systems were the most productive. As to what he considered to be the ideal system Likert maintained that organization should adopt a participative system order to achieve the highest levels of effectiveness, productivity, and satisfaction among managers and employees.

Blake and Mouton's Grid Theory

In the early 1960s Robert Blake and Jane Moulton developed a framework for categorizing and describing leadership styles that focused on two behavioral dimensions—concern for people ("people orientation") and concern for production ("production orientation" or "task orientation").[11] In contrast to many of the other leadership/management theories, Blake and Mouton did not opine as to whether it was better for a leader to be production-oriented or people-oriented (or a combination of the two) and their main interest was in establishing a model that described various leadership styles so that leaders could see where they fit and take steps to develop skills needed to adapt their styles to the wide range of circumstances that can arise during the course of managing the activities of an organizational unit.

Blake and Moulton devised the Managerial Grid, sometimes referred to as the Leadership Grid, with the dimensions referred to earlier as the two axes and each axis ranging from low on one end to high on the other. A leader's "concern for people" was measured by how much the leader considered the needs and interests of team members, as well as their personal development, when making decisions about how to accomplish tasks needed for the organization to achieve its objectives. A leader's "concern of production" was measured by the weight that the leader gave to concrete objectives, organizational efficiency, and achieving high productivity when making decisions about how to accomplish organizational tasks. Using these dimensions Blake and Moulton originally identified the following five leadership styles:

1. Country Club Leadership (High Concern for People/Low Concern for Production): A leader using this style is extremely concerned about the needs, feelings, and development of subordinates and generally assumes that as long as subordinates are feeling satisfied and secure they will be motivated to work hard to achieve the organization's production requirements. The by-product of this style, also referred to as "accommodating," tends be a comfortable work environment yet one in which production goals are often missed because of inadequate controls.

---

[11] See Blake, R., and J. Mouton. 1964. *The Managerial Grid: The Key to Leadership Excellence*. Houston: Gulf Publishing Co., and Blake, R., and J. Mouton. 1985. *The Managerial Grid III: The Key to Leadership Excellence*. Houston: Gulf Publishing Co.

2. Produce or Perish Leadership (Low Concern for People/High Concern for Production): Leaders using this style—sometimes referred to as authoritarian or dictatorial leaders—do not value the needs and feelings of subordinates and see them only as tools to be used as necessary in order to achieve production goals. The workplace environment is quite autocratic with subordinates subject to strict rules, policies, and procedures. Subordinates are motivated by fear of punishment for failing to comply as opposed to rewards for achieving their goals. This style is similar to McGregor's Theory X and is often used when organizations are in crisis.

3. Impoverished Leadership (Low Concern for People/Low Concern for Production): Not surprisingly, a leader using this style is extremely ineffective as he or she has no concern about positively motivating or satisfying his or her subordinates for creating systems and process that promote achieving of production goals. As a result, the workplace operating under impoverished leadership is chaotic and stressful for all who are a part of it. This style is sometimes referred to as "indifferent."

4. Middle-of-the-Road Leadership (Medium Concern for People/ Medium Concern for Production): This style of leadership represents an effort to compromise by not being too extreme on either of the dimensions and striking a balance between people and production concerns. The by-product of such a decision, however, is an organization that is no better than average with respect to employee satisfaction and productivity and thus unable to generate the inertia necessary for long-term sustainability and growth. In some instances leaders adopt this style (sometimes aptly referred to as the "status quo") because they doubt that their workers have the skills necessary to perform much better than average.

5. Team Leadership (High Concern for People/High Concern for Production): A leader championing teamwork involves employees in making decisions about the goals and objectives of the organization and the means that should be used to achieve production requirements and establishes processes and reward systems that are designed to satisfy the personal needs of employees to motivate them toward high production. Leaders and employees operate in an environment

of mutual trust and respect. This style is sometimes referred to as "sound" leadership.

Whereas Blake and Mouton wanted to create a model for use in analyzing organizational leadership styles they did note that team leadership was, in many instances, the preferred leadership/managerial style and recommended that leaders look for ways to adapt their approach toward something that was quite similar to McGregor's Theory Y and other participatory leadership/management styles.[12]

Transformational and Transactional Leadership

The terms "transformational leadership" and "transactional leadership" were first used by James MacGregor Burns in 1978.[13] Burns began by defining leadership as "leaders inducing followers to act for certain goals that represent the values and the motivations—the wants and needs, the aspirations and expectations—of both leaders and followers." For Burns, leaders had the greatest impact on their followers when they were able to "motivate followers to action by appealing to shared values and by satisfying the higher order needs of the led, such as their aspirations and expectations." He went on to say that "… transforming leadership ultimately becomes moral in that it raises the level of human conduct and ethical aspiration of both leader and the led, and thus it has a transforming effect on both." Although Burns clearly had feelings about the value of

---

[12] Two other styles—opportunistic and paternalistic—were added to this Grid Theory by other researchers many years after Blake and Mouton first published their work. Opportunistic leaders do not really fit into any of the initial five style categories and tend to vary their behavior to suit the current situation and achieve what is in their own personal interest. Opportunistic leaders are seen as exploitive and manipulative. Paternalistic leaders rely on praise and support to motivate employees but are not really interested in receiving and accepting opinions from employees about changes in the way that the leader should be managing the workplace. See McKee, R., and B. Carlson. 1999. *The Power to Change.* Austin, TX: Grid International Inc.

[13] References, and quotes attributed, to Burns in this section are adapted from Burns, J.M. 1978. *Leadership* New York, NY: Harper and Row.

transformational leadership he also recognized that leaders often needed to engage in another form of leadership, which he referred to as "transactional," and which was based on transactional exchanges of value between leaders and followers; in other words, leaders offered and awarded items of value under his or her control in exchange for followers providing needed inputs such as services.

Burns and others argued that done well, transformational and transactional leadership could complement one another and that leaders needed to know and understand what type of leadership would work best in a particular situation, knowledge that evolved over time as leaders accumulated more education and experience. Bass, a disciple of Burns who became the leading champion of transformational leadership in the 1990s, wrote with this colleague: "The best leadership is both transformational and transactional. Transformational leadership augments the effectiveness of transactional leadership, it does not replace transactional leadership."[14] The bridge between the two types of leadership was further illustrated by the adaptation of Kegan's six stage developmental theory by Kuhnert and Lewis, who suggested that as leaders develop they are able to grasp and practice successively "higher order" leadership traits.[15] In the model suggested by Kuhnert and Lewis, leaders generally began at the "transactional (stage 2)" level at which the commitment of the leader and his or her followers to the organization is based primarily on a sense of reciprocity. Certain leaders are eventually able to move to the "higher-order transactional (stage 3)" level where they begin to regularly

use relational ties to motivate followers to believe work is more than the performance of certain duties for certain concrete payoffs. Followers may perform at exemplary levels with little immediate payoff in order to maintain the respect of their leader.

---

[14] Waldman, D.A., B.M. Bass, and F. Yammarino. 1990. "Adding to Contingent-Reward Behavior: The Augmenting Effect of Charismatic Leadership." *Group & Organizational Studies* 15, no. 4, pp. 381–94.

[15] References, and quotes attributed, to Kuhnert and Lewis in this section are adapted from Kuhnert, K.W., and P. Lewis. 1987. "Transactional and Transformational Leadership: A Constructive/Developmental Analysis." *Academy of Management Review* 24, no. 4, pp. 648–57.

At this level a sense of trust and respect develops between the leader and his or her followers and they begin to forge an alliance that is based on mutual support, promises, expectations, obligations, and rewards. Bass noted, however, that "[a]lthough followers who are persuaded by higher level transactional leaders may expend extraordinary effort to maintain a certain level of mutual regard with their leader, their beliefs and goals typically have not changed."[16] It is the eventual integration of the leader's goals and values by his or her followers that sets the stage for the "transformational (stage 4)" level in the Kuhnert and Lewis continuum. At this level, Bass said, "… leaders are able to take an objective view of their goals and commitments; they can operate from a personal value system that transcends their agendas and loyalties."

However, although transformational and transactional leadership are related, there are clear and important distinctions between the two styles. Bass and his colleagues have demonstrated that there are meaningful distinctions between these two styles of leadership.[17] Raza explained:

Transformational leadership is distinguished from transactional leadership in that it aims at innovation, while the latter is focused on planning and execution. Furthermore, transactional leadership focuses on rewards and punishments in order to achieve goals. These characteristics suggest that transformational leadership strives to create new opportunities for employees in an organization, whereas transactional style works off of an existing structure. Another distinguishing feature between the two styles is that transformational leadership aims at motivating people while transactional leadership focuses on the use of manipulation of power and authority.[18]

---

[16] Bass, B.M. 1985. *Leadership and Performance Beyond Expectations*. New York, NY: Free Press.

[17] See Bass, B.M. 1996. *A New Paradigm of Leadership: An Inquiry into Transformational Leadership*. Alexandria, VA: Army Research Institute for the Behavioral and Social Sciences. (reviewing a series of studies that support the distinction between transformational and transactional leadership).

[18] Raza, T. November 2011. *Exploring Transformational and Transactional Leadership Styles* (citing and quoting Tucker, B.A., and H. College. 2004. "The Influence

Schuster pointed out that whereas transformational leaders appealed to "higher motivation" and sought to improve the quality of life for their followers within the organization, transactional leadership was "at best a networking of power."[19]

Bass further explained that transactional leaders accomplish their goals by rewarding employees who meet expectations by providing them with rewards such as recognition, pay increases, and promotion; however, an important part of transactional leadership is that employees who fail to meet expectations will likely be penalized.[20] As noted earlier, in contrast to transformational leadership, transactional leadership focuses on specific benefits that followers would receive by taking on and completing agreed-upon tasks, and leaders using the transactional leadership style should expect to engage in ongoing negotiations with their followers regarding the terms upon which the followers would be willing to exchange their labor for the benefits offered by the leader. The "behaviors" that are generally associated with transactional leadership are quite different than those associated with transformational leadership and include techniques and practices such as "contingent reward" and "management by exception."[21]

Raza noted that transactional leadership becomes particularly unappealing when the leader relies too heavily on "passive management by exception," which Howell and Avolio explained happens "when leaders transact with followers by focusing on mistakes, delaying decisions, or

---

of the Transformational Leader." *Journal of Leadership and Organizational Studies* 10, no. 4, pp. 103–111.)

[19] Schuster, J. 1994. "Transforming Your Leadership Style." *Association Management* 46, no. 1, p. 103.

[20] Bass, B.M. Winter 1990. "From Transactional to Transformational Leadership Learning to Share the Vision." *Organizational Dynamics*, pp. 19–31.

[21] Ardichvili, A., and K. Kuchinke. 2002. "Leadership Styles and Cultural Values Among Managers and Subordinates: A Comparative Study of Four Countries of the Former Soviet Union, Germany and the US." *Human Resource Development International* 5, no. 1, pp. 99–117, 101. (citing Bass, B.M. 1985. *Leadership and Performance Beyond Expectations*. New York, NY: The Free Press. The behaviors associated with transactional leadership are measured with the Multifactor Leadership Questionnaire.) See Avolio, B., B.M. Bass, and D. Jung. 1995. *MLQ: Multifactor Leadership Questionnaire: Technical Report*. Palo Alto, CA: Mind Garden.

avoiding intervening until something has gone wrong, or rewards focused on recognizing the work accomplished."[22] Transactional leadership is often criticized as merely a system of rewards and penalties that fails to inspire and motivate followers to do anything more than the basics of their jobs, and leaders relying on the transactional style have been accused of excess reliance on coercive, rather than referent, power and being unwilling to interact with followers unless the followers have failed to meet expectations and/or follow standards and procedures established by the leader without input from the followers.[23]

A number of researchers have claimed to have found evidence confirming the effectiveness of transformational leadership. For example, Judge and Piccolo and Stewart claimed to have found a positive correlation between team performance and the use of transformational leadership style.[24] Barling et al. found that transformational leadership facilitated a positive change in the way that followers perceived their managers and help to improve the organizational commitment and performance of the followers.[25] Lowe et al. argued that their research supported the notion that transformational leadership has a positive influence on work unit effectiveness at all levels of the organization and that leaders would do well to focus on engaging their followers and providing

---

[22] Howell, J., and B. Avolio. 1993. "Transformational Leadership, Transactional Leadership, Locus of Control and Support for Innovation: Key Predictors of Consolidated-Business-Unit Performance." *Journal of Applied Psychology* 78, no. 6, p. 891.

[23] Bass, B.M. Winter 1997. "From Transactional to Transformational Leadership Learning to Share the Vision." *Understanding the dynamics of power and influence in organizations*, pp. 19–31; and Jayasingam, S., and M.A. Ansari, and M. Jantan. 2010. "Influencing Knowledge Workers: The Power of Top Management." *Industrial Management and Data Systems* 110, no. 1, pp. 134–51.

[24] Judge, T., and R. Piccolo. 2004. "Transformational and Transactional Leadership: A Meta-Analytic Test of their Relative Validity." *Journal of Applied Psychology* 89, no. 5, pp. 755–68; Stewart, G. 2006. "A Meta-Analytic Review of Relationships Between Team Design Features and Team Performance." *Journal of Management* 32, no. 1, pp. 29–54.

[25] Barling, J., T. Weber, and E. Kelloway. 1996. "Effects of Transformational Leadership Training on Attitudinal Financial Outcomes: A Field Experiment." *Journal of Applied Psychology* 81, no. 6, p. 872.

them with individual consideration.[26] Other researchers have identified a positive relationship between transformational leadership and financial performance whereas simultaneously finding that transactional leadership style, with its excessive emphasis on meeting goals and achieving desired results, negatively impacts unit performance and caused followers to lose motivation and feel that their freedom to grow within the organization was limited.[27] Wells and Peachey suggested that the engaging style of transformational leaders would lead to more meaningful and satisfying relationships between followers and their organization and thus reduce the likelihood that the followers would leave and seek jobs elsewhere.[28]

If one assumes the validity of the distinction between transformational and transactional leadership and the value of transformational leadership in certain instances, the key question then becomes: How can leaders effectively motivate their followers to accept the transformational style? Bass and Steidlmeir offered four interrelated components that were explained by Homrig as follows[29]:

---

[26] Lowe, B., G. Kroeck, and N. Sivasubramanium. 1996. "Effectiveness Correlates of Transformational and Transactional Leadership: A Meta-Analytic Review of the MLQ Literature." *Leadership Quarterly* 7, no. 3, pp. 385–425.

[27] Howell, J., and B. Avolio. 1993. "Transformational Leadership, Transactional Leadership, Locus of Control and Support for Innovation: Key Predictors of Consolidated-Business-Unit Performance." *Journal of Applied Psychology* 78, no. 6, p. 891; Barling, J., T. Weber, and E. Kelloway. 1996. "Effects of Transformational Leadership Training on Attitudinal Financial Outcomes: A Field Experiment." *Journal of Applied Psychology* 81, no. 6, p. 872; Judge, T., and R. Piccolo. 2004. "Transformational and Transactional Leadership: A Meta-Analytic Test of their Relative Validity." *Journal of Applied Psychology* 89, no. 5, pp. 755–68; and Bass, B.M., D. Jung, B. Avolio, and Y. Berson. 2003. "Predicting Unit Performance by Assessing Transformational and Transactional Leadership." *Journal of Applied Psychology* 88, no. 2, pp. 207–18.

[28] Wells, J., and W. Peachey. 2010. "Turnover Intentions: Do Leadership Behaviours and Satisfaction with Leader Matters?" *Team Performance Management* 17, nos. ½, pp. 23–40.

[29] Homrig, M. December 21, 2001. "Transformational Leadership." http://leadership.au.af.mil/documents/homrig.htm (accessed December 14, 2018) (adapting from Bass, B.M., and P. Steidlmeier. 1998. *Ethics, Character and Authentic Transformational Leadership*. On authentic leadership, see George, B. et al. 2017.

1. Idealized influence, which calls for building genuine trust between leaders and followers based on a solid moral and ethical foundation. Bass explained: "If the leadership is truly transformational, its charisma or idealized influence is characterized by high moral and ethical standards."

2. Inspirational motivation, which occurs when the leader's appeal to what is right and needs to be done serves as the impetus and motivator for the activities of the followers. Bass explained: "Its [transformational leadership's] inspirational motivation provides followers with challenges and meaning for engaging in shared goals and undertakings."[30]

3. Intellectual stimulation, which Bass explained "… helps followers to question assumptions and to generate more creative solutions to problems." The ability of followers to question assumptions and think creatively is built on the leader's success in providing them with a sense of the "big picture" and the leader's vision with respect to the organization, the connections between everyone in the organization, and the overall goals of the organization.

4. Individual consideration, which Bass explained occurred when a leader "… treats each follower as an individual and provides coaching, mentoring and growth opportunities." This component stresses the need for leaders to recognize and fulfill the needs of their followers with respect to self-actualization, self-fulfillment, and self-worth, and the success of the leader is essential to motivating followers toward greater achievement and further growth.

Homrig himself also offered a summary of the ingredients for transformational leadership that he had recognized through his extensive review of the research: Leaders have high moral and ethical values; leaders express genuine interest in followers; leaders have an inspirational vision; genuine trust exists between leaders and the led; followers share leader's values and vision; leaders and followers perform beyond self-interest; participatory

---

Authentic Leadership (HBR Emotional Intelligence Series). Cambridge MA: Harvard Business Press.)

[30] For guidance on acting as an inspirational leader, see Garton, E. April 25, 2017. "How to Be an Inspiring Leader." *Harvard Business Review.*

decision-making is the rule; innovative thinking and action is expected; motivation is to do the right thing; and leaders mentor. For Homrig, "… the goal of transformational leaders is to inspire followers to share the leader's values and connect with the leader's vision."

Muczyk and Reimann's Directive/Participatory Leadership Model

Muczyk and Reimann suggested that five "mainstream" North American leadership dimensions could be identified and that two of them—participation and direction—were situational or contingent, meaning that leaders could, depending on the circumstances, take different approaches to how they make decisions (i.e., the degree of participation by subordinates) and how those decisions are executed (i.e., the level of direct control over execution exercised by the leader).[31] Although "making" and "executing" decisions can be separated, as a practical matter they are obviously tightly connected and essential to the leader's overall objective of obtaining results. Muczyk and Reimann argued that it was possible and useful to construct four generic profiles of leader behavior by combining the extreme points of the two situational dimensions, thus creating four possible leadership styles for analysis: directive autocrat, permissive autocrat, directive democrat, and permissive democrat.

In a later work relying on the original Muczyk/Reimann model, Muczyk and Adler noted that the influence of societal culture has played a big part in the evolution of the debate on what constitutes effective "leadership." They pointed out that "most of the post-WWII leadership literature has been generated by American scholars"[32] and that this has

---

[31] Muczyk, J.P., and B.C. Reimann. 1987. "The Case for Directive Leadership." *The Academy of Management Executive* 1, no. 3, pp. 301–11. The description of the model is based on the discussion appearing in Muczyk, J.P., and T. Adler. 2002. "An Attempt at a Consentience Regarding Formal Leadership." *Journal of Leadership and Organizational Studies* 9, no. 2, pp. 2–17. For further discussion of situational leadership, see Blanchard, K., P. Zigarmi, and D. Zigarmi. 2013. *Leadership and the One Minute Manager Updated Ed: Increasing Effectiveness through Situational Leadership*. New York, NY: William Morrow.

[32] Muczyk, J.P., and D. Holt. May 2008. "Toward a Cultural Contingency Model of Leadership." *Journal of Leadership & Organizational Studies* 14,

led to prescriptions that leaders everywhere should act in ways preferred and celebrated in American culture, which meant practicing democratic leadership and supporting individual autonomy. Muczyk and Adler also suggested that the notion of "soft power"—described by Ikeda as the reliance on knowledge and information, shared values, ideas, and international law as opposed to reliance on military might, formal authority, and wealth[33]—had a strong influence on popularization of leadership models that were "non-positional, team based, or empowerment centered." However, Muczyk and Adler cautioned that "the leadership construct should not be a peculiarly American one" and should instead be "universal." They went on to argue that the only way to formulate a useful universal leadership construct was to present it in a "contingency/situational framework" that accounted for things such as societal culture, which often required that leaders incorporate autocratic and directive elements into their styles when operating in societies outside of the United States,[34] and the characteristics of subordinates, business practices, and business strategies.[35]

---

no. 4, pp. 277–286, 277. (citing Nadler, N. 2002. *International Dimensions of Organizational Behavior*, 4th ed. Cincinnati, OH: Southwestern); and Koopman, P.L., D.N. Den Hartog, and E. Konrad. 1999. "National Culture and Leadership Profiles in Europe: Some results from the GLOBE Study." *European Journal of Work and Organizational Psychology* 8, no. 4, pp. 503–20.

[33] Ikeda, D. November 1991. "The Age of "Soft Power" and Inner-Motivated Philosophy." *New Century*, pp. 9–15 (cited in Muczyk, J.P., and T. Adler. 2002. "An Attempt at a Consentience Regarding Formal Leadership." *Journal of Leadership and Organizational Studies* 9, no. 2, pp. 2–17). Muczyk and Adler also referred to several articles that they believed reflected the influence of "soft power" on recommendations about how leaders should act, including "Leading From the Grass Roots," "Creating Organizations with Many Leaders," and "The Leader Who Serves."

[34] For further discussion of impact of societal culture on the choice of the most effective leadership style in the Muczyk/Adler model, see "Cross-Cultural Leadership Studies" prepared and distributed by the Sustainable Entrepreneurship Project (www.seproject.org).

[35] Muczyk, J.P., and T. Adler. 2002. "An Attempt at a Consentience Regarding Formal Leadership." *Journal of Leadership and Organizational Studies* 9, no. 2, pp. 2–17. A well-studied example of when autocratic or directive behavior from the organizational leader is required as a matter of "business strategy" is in situations where the organization is in need of a "turnaround" or "retrenchment."

Directive Autocrat

The "directive autocrat" style features no employee participation in decision-making and extensive directive behavior or follow-up on execution. Although this type of style sounds particularly extreme in countries such as the United States, where democratic and permissive leadership approaches are generally preferred and lauded, Muczyk and Adler explained that this type of leader

> is not some misanthrope or ogre, but merely a person who is paid to make the important decisions, set the salient goals, and direct subordinates along the way—especially in a crisis, when subordinates tend to rally around a decisive leader.[36]

A directive autocratic is the preferred type of leader in situation that require quick action and there is no time for extensive consultation or consensus building among subordinates and Muczyk and Adler observed that this leadership style is probably appropriate when subordinates are new, inexperienced, and/or underqualified. A directive autocratic approach is also needed when there is an adversarial relationship between managers and employers and the organizational leader has no choice but to coerce workers into doing their jobs. In order to be effective, however, a directive autocrat must have extensive knowledge of the organizational mission and must be comfortable acting in an autocratic fashion. The directive autocrat must not forget that he or she must still treat people with courtesy, dignity, and respect and, in fact, evidence indicates that if such a leader follows this simple advice he or she will be perceived much more positively than one might expect.[37] One method for making the

---

[36] Id. Other research has provided evidence to support the notion that autocratic and directive behavior is especially needed in "turnaround" or "retrenchment" situations in order to ensure that the organization is able to achieve vital goals and objectives in a time of crisis. See, e.g., Muczyk, J.P., and R. Steel. March-April 1998. "Leadership Style and the Turnaround Executive." *Business Horizons*, pp. 39–46.

[37] Muczyk and Adler, referencing the previously cited research done by Muczyk and Steel, noted several instances where autocratic and directive leaders achieved

"medicine go down easier" is to mix direction with tools that enable subordinates, such as training in the new technologies that may be necessary in order for the organization to succeed.

Permissive Autocrat

The "permissive autocrat" style features no employee participation in decision-making and no directive behavior or follow-up on execution. In other words, "[t]his type of leader ... makes decisions alone, but permits followers a great deal of latitude in accomplishing their delegated tasks."[38] Like the directive autocrat style, this style is well suited for situations where quick decisions are needed but delegation of the "means to the ends" to subordinates only makes sense in situations where the tasks and activities that need to be completed are relatively simple and structured or the subordinates have the requisite levels of experience, ability, and initiative.[39] In addition, a permissive autocratic is generally willing to forego direct control if he or she has in place adequate substitutes for personal direction, which Muczyk and Adler listed as including "well-defined or routine tasks, explicit rules and procedures, technology, incentive systems, professional standards, or a strong corporate culture."[40] They cited the example of Debbi Fields, founder of Mrs. Field's Cookies, relying

---

impressive financial results in crisis situations yet were eventually dismissed by the board of directors, with the support and appreciation of employees, when it became clear that their tyrannical actions with respect to employees (e.g., public hazing, humiliation, and physical intimidation) failed to meet the requirement of treating subordinates with courtesy, dignity, and respect.

[38] Muczyk, J.P., and T. Adler. 2002. "An Attempt at a Consentience Regarding Formal Leadership." *Journal of Leadership and Organizational Studies* 9, no. 2, pp. 2–17.

[39] Muczyk and Adler noted that the "permissive autocrat" style may be suitable, and even necessary, in certain turnaround situations that call for a leader who can quickly develop his or her own broad vision for transforming the organization, because the prior strategies obviously did not work, and a group of key people who buy into the leader's vision without question and have the skills and experience to expertly execute the strategies associated with the leader's vision without an excessive amount of direct control. Id.

[40] Id.

on an in-store expert information system to control operational aspects of every franchised store and track whether the managers of those stores were following the directives issued from the top of the organization by comparing store performance against standards programmed into the information system.[41]

Directive Democrat

The "directive democrat" style features both extensive employee participation in decision-making and extensive directive behavior or follow-up on execution. In other words, subordinates are very involved in the decision-making process but once the decision is made the leader closely supervises the subordinates to make sure they are properly completing their assigned tasks. Muczyk and Adler suggest that this style is appropriate when the project is complex and involves many interdependent activities. In this situation, the speed of the decision is generally less important than making sure that the solution chosen is technically correct and the chances of arriving at such a solution increase with broader input from those who will be involved in the project. The need for close supervision arises when the subordinates lack either experience or ability or the leader feels that they are not reliable and will not take the initiative on their own to get the project completed as planned.

Permissive Democrat

The "permissive democrat" style features extensive employee participation in decision-making and no directive behavior or follow-up on execution. In other words, a great situation for subordinates who have an opportunity to participate in making decisions and setting goals and autonomy to decide for themselves the best way to execute the decisions that they helped to make. According to Muczyk and Adler, this style works well in organizations where involving subordinates has both information and motivational benefits; however, they caution that such an approach will

---

[41] Id. (citing Cash, J.I., F.W. McFarlan, J.L. McKenney, and L. Applegate. 1992. *Corporate Information Systems Management*. Homewood, IL: Irwin.)

be successful only if certain conditions are satisfied, such as highly qualified employees, effective substitutes for personal direction, and sufficient
time to seek opinion and reach a consensus. A permissive democratic
must also genuinely value the democratic process and have faith and
trust in the judgment of his or her subordinates and their capabilities and
motivations with respect to completing the necessary tasks and activities.

Evolution of Leadership Styles

Having suggested and described their four leadership styles, Muczyk and
Adler then turned their attention to examining whether one particular
style would be best for the entire lifecycle of the organization or whether
changes in the leadership style would be required as the organization
evolves through various stages of development. They noted that several
researchers had concluded that changes in leadership style do occur as
time goes by and suggested a "leadership cycle" for organizations that pro-
ceeded from "directive autocrat" during the early stages of organizational
development to "permissive democrat" by the time that organizations
become more mature and sophisticated.[42] Although Muczyk and Adler
conceded that it was possible for an organization to jump immediately
from a directive autocrat to a permissive democrat, the more likely sce-
nario was a gradual change of just one of the dimensions at a time—for
example, a directive autocrat might first attempt to become either more
participative, perhaps by learning to seek out the opinions of subordinates

---

[42] Id. It is also possible for this type of evolution to occur in very large organizations that are confronted with a crisis that dictates the temporary use of the
"directive autocratic" style during a turnaround phase followed by a turn to a
less autocratic approach once the necessary drastic changes have been made and
the restructured organization is running more smoothly. Muczyk and Adler
cited the example of Jack Welch as CEO of General Electric, who initially acted
in ways described as "ruthless" to reduce the number of employees, eliminate
management positions, and shut down entire business units and then eventually
announced, once the purging was completed and the organization had returned
to financial success, that "there was no room at GE for autocrats." See Muczyk,
J.P., and R. Steel. March-April 1998. "Leadership Style and the Turnaround
Executive." *Business Horizons*, pp. 39–46.

more often, or less directive by recruiting new mid-level managers that he or she could come to trust to handle execution of decisions. Muczyk and Adler suggest that the transition generally begins by opening up the decision-making process to a wider range of people (i.e., moving from "autocrat" to "democrat") followed by more and more delegation of the finer points of execution to subordinates as they become more familiar with the goals and purposes of the activities through their participation in the original decision. The transition from directive to permissive can also be eased through the use of the substitutes for personal direction discussed earlier.[43]

Emotional Intelligence and Leadership Styles

Goleman is also among the army of researchers looking for the elusive answer to the seemingly simple and basic question: "What should leaders do?"[44] His answer was that "the leader's singular job is to get results" and he argued that it was possible to use the results of quantitative research to identify those "leadership behaviors" that would produce the most positive results. Based on the research data that he reviewed, Goleman believed that the best leaders were able to mix and match the competencies associated with emotional intelligence to suit the particular challenges and problems they were confronting at any point in time and argued that six basic leadership styles could be identified among leaders of knowledge workers that were based on various combinations of the competencies

---

[43] Muczyk and Adler did not dismiss the possibility that a directive autocrat might attempt to initiate change by recruiting capable and independent employees who could support a "permissive" approach to control while the leader continued to make the decisions without input; however, Muczyk and Adler commented that it might be difficult for such a leader to attract and retain those types of employees because they presumably would grow weary of not being allowed to participate in key decisions using the knowledge that they had gained through their responsibilities in executing the strategies set in the past.

[44] Goleman is well known for his argument that a high level of "emotional intelligence" is necessary for effective leadership, a subject that is discussed in detail in "Leadership Traits and Attributes" prepared and distributed by the Sustainable Entrepreneurship Project (www.seproject.org).

of emotional intelligence: "coercive," often also referred to as "directive" or "commanding"; "authoritative," often also referred to as "visionary"; "affiliative"; "democratic"; "pacesetting"; and "coaching."[45] In Goleman's view, the best leaders not only needed emotional intelligence but also skill and acumen at identifying and applying the appropriate leadership style for the situation. The following is a brief summary of each of these styles using some of Goleman's own words and elaborations provided by others[46]:

- The "coercive" leader develops strategies and ideas largely without input or consultation and then issues clear directions that he or she expects to be followed immediately and without challenge (i.e., "Do what I tell you!" and "Just do it!") and uses a style based on the emotional intelligence competencies of a drive to achieve, initiative, and self-control. A coercive leader often appears to be cold and distant and exudes emotional self-control which hopefully serves as a calming influence that also gives members of the group confidence that the leader is moving the group in the right direction. This style is best suited to crisis situations where immediate action is required to launch a turnaround and may also be adopted with problem members of the group when other leadership styles have failed to motivate them. This style, which is sometimes also referred to as "directive" or "commanding," can lead to problems when group members are already competent and motivated on their own to perform and succeed.

- The "authoritative" or "visionary" leader mobilizes people toward a shared vision by providing a picture of where the

---

[45] Goleman, D. March-April 2000. "Leadership That Gets Results." *Harvard Business Review* 78, no. 2, pp. 4–17.

[46] Id. at pp. 82–83 ("The Six Leadership Styles at a Glance").Elaborations are drawn from Goleman, D., A. McKee, and R. Boyatzis. 2002. Primal Leadership: Realizing the Power of Emotional Intelligence. Cambridge, MA: Harvard Business Press; and Richard, L., and M. Sirkin. December 2008. "Six Styles: How Will You Handle Your Firm's Reins?" Law Practice, pp. 32–34.

group should be going but not telling them exactly how they should get there (i.e., "Come with me") and uses a style based on the emotional intelligence competencies of self-confidence, empathy, and change catalyst. A visionary leader is authoritative rather than authoritarian and excels at providing information to the group that can be used in order to navigate the path to the desired end result. A visionary leader is particularly good at explaining to members of the group how their contributions will assist the group in achieving its goals and objectives. This style works best when organizational changes require a "new vision" or when it is necessary for the leader to set a clear direction for the organization and may not be successful when the group to be motivated includes more experienced experts or peers.

- The "affiliative" leader focuses on building connections and emotional bonds between people within the group (i.e., "People come first") in an effort to create harmony that is conducive to strong levels of collaboration and uses a style based on the emotional intelligence competencies of empathy, building relationships, and communication. An affiliative leader emphasizes emotional needs over the specific tasks needed to complete particular work activities. This style improves morale and reduces conflicts and generally has a positive impact on the group culture and work environment, particularly during times when the group is experiencing high levels of stress and/or is trying to heal internal rifts, and is well suited to supporting the principles of a visionary leader; however, an affiliative leader may have difficulty in taking necessary action that might lead to emotional distress such as delivering negative feedback to members of the group.

- The "democratic" leader forges consensus through participation (i.e., asking people "What do you think?") and uses a style based on the emotional intelligence competencies of collaboration, team leadership, and communication. A democratic leader works hard to elicit inputs from all parts of the group through participation and simply listening to reports from group members. A democratic leader seeks both good and bad news and makes an effort to demonstrate that the information provided is valued and used in making decisions about the direction of the group and the way that the work flow is structured. This type of leadership style is sometimes referred to as "participative" and practitioners are noted for their ability to be a good listener and a team player and their skills in influencing others to take the necessary actions and commit themselves to the goals set by the leader. This style has a positive impact on the group culture and work environment and works best when the leader needs to obtain "buy-in" to a chosen strategic direction or a consensus from subordinates or to solicit input or collect missing information from key employees to make a decision. A democratic leader must not, however, get bogged down in listening and must demonstrate that he or she can also act decisively based on the information collected.

- The "pacesetting" leader leads by setting challenging and exciting goals for members of the group and pushing them to succeed by establishing expectations of high-level performance (i.e., "Do as I do, now") and uses a style based on the emotional intelligence competencies of conscientiousness, drive to achieve, and initiative. A pacesetting leader is generally willing to lead by example and step in to complete an activity when others are having difficulties; however, this type of leader often fails to provide group members with the basic training and guidance necessary for them to be successful on their own. A group with a pacesetting leader often experiences good short-term results but as time goes by frustration builds and the impact on the group culture and work environment can become quite negative. A pacesetting leader may be innovative and highly creative in his or her own area of expertise—with high standards for his or her own performance—yet have little or no understanding of how to teach or motivate others. This style works best where the members of the group are already highly motivated and have acquired the necessary level of competence from other sources and experiences.

- The "coaching" leader focuses on developing people for the future (i.e., "Try this") and uses a style based on the emotional intelligence competencies of developing others, empathy, and self-awareness. A coaching leader spends a good deal of time and effort identifying the wants and aspirations of members of the group and then connecting those desires to the goals that have been established for the group. A coaching leader will meet with people in the group to determine their strengths and weaknesses and then use this information to find the best organizational roles for them. A coaching leader is willing to delegate assignments and authority, a practice which motivates people to succeed in order to justify the faith that the leader has placed in them. This style, which is also sometimes referred to as "mentoring," is best suited to situations where members of the group need to improve performance or build long-term strengths and capabilities and can have a positive impact on the group culture and work environment; however, a coaching leader must take care not to engage in micromanaging.

Goleman's research also uncovered evidence that he believed supported the conclusion that each style had a direct and unique impact on what he referred to as the "organizational climate" of the company, division, or team that was being led and, in turn, on the results that the leader was able to achieve in terms of financial performance. Goleman explained that the "organizational climate" consisted of six key factors that influenced the working environment of the company, division, or team, including such things as flexibility (i.e., the freedom afforded to employees to innovate without worrying about restrictions and authorizations ("red tape")); the sense of responsibility that employees feel toward the organization; the level of standards set for activities within the organization; the sense of accuracy about performance feedback and aptness of rewards for performance; the level of clarity that organizational members have regarding the overall mission and values of the organization;

and the level of commitment among members of the organization toward pursuing and achieving a common purpose.[47] Goleman's analysis of the data showed a correlation between each leadership style and each aspect of organizational climate and he found that the overall impact of the "authoritative" style on the organizational climate was "most strongly positive," the highest endorsement among the six styles. The "affiliative," "democratic," and "coaching" styles each had a "positive impact" on climate, whereas the "coercive" and "pacesetting" styles both had a "negative impact" on climate. Goleman concluded that no style should be relied on exclusively and that each style, even those that had a "negative impact" on climate, had at least short-term uses that made them appropriate for specific issues and challenges that the leader had to address at a given moment.[48]

Researchers go to great lengths to emphasize that the six categories described earlier are styles of leadership rather than leadership types and that leaders can make a conscious choice to adopt, or avoid, a particular leadership style and can also deploy a mix of two or more styles at any given point in time in order to fit the particular circumstances and environmental challenges currently confronting the organization. Goleman argued that leaders could be trained, through hard work, to expand their "style repertories," just as they could improve their abilities with respect to the competencies associated with emotional intelligence. Although it is not clear that persons with particular personality traits can vary their leadership styles as easily as one might like, it does make sense for leaders to realize that there is more than just one way to motivate their followers

---

[47] Goleman, D. March-April 2000. "Leadership that Gets Results." *Harvard Business Review*, pp. 78–90, 81.

[48] Id. ("Getting Molecular: The Impact of Leadership Styles on Drivers of Climate"). The table in the article allows readers to see the correlations between the leadership styles and each of the climatic factors. For example, predictably the "coercive" and "democratic" styles had very different impacts on the measured level of "flexibility" in the organizational climate. In addition, the results showed that there were varying levels of correlation for each style with respect to the various climatic factors: For the "authoritative" style, there was a strongly positive correlation with respect to "rewards" but a decidedly weaker correlation, albeit still positive, to "responsibility."

and drive the organization firm in a direction that makes sense for everyone involved. The key question, of course, is identifying which of the leadership styles are best suited for a particular leader and the situation that he or she is dealing with at any given time.

In addition, leaders could build a team that includes members adept at employing styles that the leader lacks. For example, a leader who prefers, and is good at, building personal relationships with employees (i.e., the "affiliative" style) could delegate performance standards to a member of the leader's management team whose strengths with respect to emotional intelligence competencies include self-confidence, empathy, and change catalyst and thus made him or her more suited to applying the "authoritative" style necessary for crystallizing the vision necessary for the organization to achieve the desired results. Goleman mentioned that this particular situation also called for a manager who could serve as a "pacesetter" to support the establishment and pursuit of high performance standards.[49]

Even if leaders can and do develop the ability to effectively deploy two or more of the leadership styles, he or she will not be effective unless the style is suitable and appropriate for the particular organizational context. For example, it is generally accepted that the "authoritative" and "coaching" styles are particularly well suited to knowledge workers and that the "affiliative" and "democratic" styles are also appropriate for such workers although probably best when deployed with the first two styles. On the other hand, "pacesetting" and "coercive" styles are only recommended and effective in very specific situations and then only for a short period of time. If a leader continues to use a "pacesetting" or "coercive" style for an extended period he or she can expect a decided downturn in organizational performance and morale and eventually drive the organization's best managers and workers—including those who are highly skilled in other leadership styles in their own right—to seek other places to work.

Farkas and Wetlaufer's "Approaches to Leadership"

Farkas and Wetlaufer believed that the behavior of leaders could be analyzed and categorized by their "approach to leadership," which they

---

[49] Id. at pp. 89–90.

described as the leader's "guiding, overarching philosophy about how he or she can best add value."[50] Specifically, "approach" meant

> which areas of corporate policy—for example, strategic planning, R&D, or recruiting—receive the most attention, what kind of people and behaviors the CEO values in the organization, which decisions the CEO makes personally or delegates, and how he or she spends each day.

Although Farkas and Wetlaufer referred often to "leadership" in their work, in fact they were toiling their results were a better fit for identification and explanation of managerial roles and, in fact, they commented that "a leadership approach is a coherent, explicit style of management." Farkas and Wetlaufer did not discount the importance and relevance of the personality traits of the leader; however, they argued that the most effective leaders, based on the CEOs that they studied, did not simply adopt the leadership approach that was the best fit for their personalities but instead opted for the approach that was best for the organization in light of the competitive challenges confronting the organization, the potential competitive advantages available to the organization, and the organization's resources (i.e., capital, technology, and people). Based on interviews with 160 CEOs in different countries and industries, Farkas and Wetlaufer identified the following five "leadership approaches"[51]:

1. The "strategy" approach is used by the CEO who is primarily focused on creating, testing, and designing the implementation of a long-term strategy for the organization and this type of leader spends a good deal of time on identifying and understanding the organization's current business situation and developing a vision for the desired future situation and the path to get there.
2. The "human-assets" approach is used by the CEO who is most concerned about imparting to his or her organization "certain values,

---

[50] Farkas, C., and S. Wetlaufer. May-June 1996. "The Ways Chief Executives Lead." *Harvard Business Review*, pp. 110–22.
[51] Id.

behaviors, and attitudes by closely managing the growth and development of individuals." In this instance, the CEO spends a lot of time traveling to meet personally with individuals within the organization and invests a good deal of his or her effort in "personnel-related activities such as recruiting, performance reviews, and career mapping."

3. The "expertise" approach features a CEO obsession with identifying and nurturing those sources of expertise within the organization that can serve as the basis for a competitive advantage. For example, the CEO will devote most of his or her time to studying and understanding new technologies, analyzing competitor's products, and meeting with customers and engineers to get their views of where the industry is moving. The CEO will seek to motivate and encourage others to join him or her in this quest by creating and championing programs that train people to pursue innovation and reward them for ideas and systems that contribute to creation of a competitive advantage.

4. The "box" approach features the creation and use of an explicit set of financial, operational, and cultural controls to "ensure uniform, predictable behaviors and experiences for customers and employees." The CEO who uses this approach is predisposed to favoring detailed, prescriptive policies and procedures and establishing reward systems that are tied to compliance with those policies and procedures. A good deal of the CEOs time is spent on understanding and resolving "exceptions" to the controls and budgets that have been established, such as understanding why projected financial targets have not been attained. Farkas and Wetlaufer noted that the CEOs using this approach tended to prefer using a seniority-based system for promotion.

5. The "change" approach is used by a CEO who believes that his or her role is to create an environment of continuous change, or "reinvention," in order for the organization to survive in an environment that is also changing dramatically all the time. Many of the tools used by other types of CEOs—strategic plans, control systems, policies, and procedures—are rarely used by a "change" CEO and he or she spends most of his time in meetings with employees from all over

the organization pitching a "gestalt" of change. Farkas and Wetlaufer comment that this approach often leads to chaos within the organization and strategic miscues.

GLOBE Project

The Global Leadership and Organizational Behavior Effectiveness project, commonly referred to as "GLOBE," was conceived and launched in the early 1990s by Robert J. House and is considered to be the most extensive and ambitious attempt to gather and analyze information relevant to the study of the cross-cultural aspects of leadership.[52] The data used for the GLOBE project were first collected from 1994 to 1997 by 170 voluntary collaborators around the world ("country co-investigators") who administered written surveys to about 17,000 managers from nearly 1,000 local (i.e., non-multinational) organizations in 62 different countries. The original focus of the GLOBE project was studying the perceptions of leadership among the participants in the survey and the GLOBE researchers defined leadership as "... the ability of an individual to influence, motivate, and enable others to contribute toward the effectiveness and success of the organizations of which they are members."[53]

The GLOBE leadership questionnaires included over 100 behavioral and attribute descriptors that the survey designers hypothesized as either contributing to a person's ability to be an outstanding leader or inhibited

---

[52] For an interesting and detailed overview of the development of the GLOBE project and the organizational processes used to collect and analyze the information, see House, R., and N. Mansor. 1999. "Cultural Influences on Leadership and Organizations." *I Advances in Global Leadership*, pp. 171–233.

[53] House, R., P. Hanges, M. Javidan, P. Dorfman, and V. Gupta, eds. 2004. *Culture, Leadership, and Organizations: The GLOBE Study of 62 Societies* 15. The GLOBE researchers were careful to point out that the definition they used pertained to "organizational leadership" and not to leadership in general and noted that others had suggested broader definitions of leadership that might apply in other contexts (e.g., political leaders) such as a "group member whose influence on group attitudes, performance, or decision making greatly exceeds that of the average member of the group." See Simonton, D. 1994. *Greatness: Who Makes History and Why*, 411.

a person's ability to be an outstanding leader. Each of the participants were asked to rate each of the descriptors on a scale of one to seven with a rating of one meaning that the behavior or attribute greatly inhibited a person from being an outstanding leader and a rating of seven meaning that the behavior or attribute greatly contributed to a person being an outstanding leader.[54] Following analysis and verification of the responses to the leadership questionnaires, the GLOBE researchers concluded that there was substantial statistical support for the following "culturally endorsed" implicit theories of leadership (i.e., leadership styles)[55]:

- Charismatic/Value-Based Leadership: This style is based on the ability of a leader to inspire, to motivate, and to expect high performance from others based on strongly held core values. Key behavioral attributes associated with this type of leadership style include being visionary, inspirational, self-sacrificing, trustworthy, decisive, and performance oriented.
- Team-Oriented Leadership: This style reflects an emphasis on team building and defining and establishing a common purpose among team members. Key behavioral attributes associated with this type of leadership style include being collaborative, integrative, diplomatic, nonmalevolent, and administratively competent.
- Participative Leadership: This style reflects the willingness and ability of the leader to involve others in making and implementing decisions. Key behavioral attributes associated with this type of leadership style include being participative and nonautocratic.
- Humane-Oriented Leadership: This style reflects an emphasis on the leader's ability to be supportive, considerate, compassionate, and generous to his or her followers. Key behavioral attributes associated with this type of leadership style include modesty and sensitivity to people.

---

[54] Dickson, M.W., D.N. Den Hartog, and J.K. Mitchelson. 2003. "Research on Leadership in a Cross-Cultural Context: Making Progress, and Raising New Questions." Leadership Quarterly 14, no. 6, pp. 752–53.

[55] Northouse, P.G. 2006. Leadership: Theory and Practice, 314, 4th ed.

- Autonomous Leadership: This style refers to leaders who act independently and individualistically. Key behavioral attributes associated with this type of leadership style include being autonomous and unique.
- Self-Protective Leadership: This style reflects an emphasis on ensuring the safety and security of the leader and his or her group. Key behavioral attributes associated with this type of leadership style include being self-centered, status conscious, conflict inducing, face saving, and procedural.

The GLOBE researchers concluded that the information collected during the survey provided evidence that the six global leadership dimensions of culturally endorsed implicit theories of leadership were significantly correlated with isomorphic dimensions of societal and organizational culture and that selected cultural differences strongly influence important ways in which people think about leaders and norms concerning the status, influence, and privileges granted to leaders.[56] For example, they found that all of the attributes associated with team-oriented leadership were universally endorsed; however, this type of approach was perceived as being especially important for effective leadership in societies where in-group collectivism, humane orientation, and uncertainty avoidance were all high such as the countries in the Southern Asian, Confucian Asian, and Latin American clusters, all of which strongly endorsed team-oriented leadership styles.[57] In addition,

---

[56] House, R.J., and N. Mansor. 1999. *Cultural Influences on Leadership and Organizations*, 1 Vols. Advances in Global Leadership 171–-233. For further discussion of the analyses of the data undertaken by the GLOBE researchers to demonstrate support for the culturally endorsed nature of the GLOBE global leadership dimensions, referred to by the researchers as "leadership scales," see also Guidelines for the Use of GLOBE Culture and Leadership Scales, August 1, 2006, available at http://bsos.umd.edu/psyc/hanges/index_files/GLOBE_Culture_and_Leadership_Scales_Guidelines.pdf

[57] Dorfman, P., P. Hanges, and F. Brodbeck. 2004. "Leadership Prototypes and Cultural Variation: The Identification of Culturally Endorsed Implicit Theories of Leadership." In *Culture, Leadership, and Organizations: The GLOBE Study of 62 Societies*, eds. R. House, P. Hanges, M. Javidan, P. Dorfman and V. Gupta. See also House, R.J., and N. Mansor. 1999. *Cultural Influences on Leadership and Organizations, I Advances in Global Leadership*, pp. 171–233.

whereas two of the attributes associated with charismatic/value-based leadership—the visionary and inspirational attributes—were universally endorsed, support for a third attribute—self-sacrifice—was mixed across cultures. The level of support for charismatic/value-based leadership was likely to be higher in societies where cultural values included strong in-group collectivism and humane orientation, such as the countries in the Anglo, Germanic, and Nordic culture clusters. Finally, whereas there was general support for humane and participative leadership, the response varied significantly across cultures and the general rule was that the intensity of endorsement of participative leadership within a country was negatively correlated with the strength of uncertainty avoidance, assertiveness, and power distance in that country. In addition, support for participative leadership was positively correlated to performance orientation and gender egalitarianism. Not surprisingly, participative leadership was most warmly embraced in the Germanic, Anglo, and Nordic cultural clusters.

Servant Leadership

Servant leadership has attracted a great deal of attention as an alternative to the traditional command and control models that have dominated leadership theories and prescriptions. The most widely quoted and accepted definition of servant leadership comes from Greenleaf, who provided the following explanation of "Who is the servant-leader?":

> The servant-leader *is* servant first…. It begins with the natural feeling that one wants to serve, to serve *first*. Then conscious choice brings one to aspire to lead. That person is sharply different from one who is *leader* first…. The difference manifests itself in the care taken by the servant-first to make sure that other people's highest priority needs are being served. The best test, and difficult to administer, is this: Do those served grow as persons? Do they, *while being served*, become healthier, wiser, freer, more autonomous, more likely themselves to become servants? *And*, what is

the effect on the least privileged in society; will they benefit, or, at least, not be further deprived?[58]

Many of the other definitions and descriptions of servant leadership strike a similar tone. For example, Archbishop Desmond Tutu explained: "The leader is the servant. So leadership is not having your own way. It's not for self-aggrandizement. But oddly, it is for service. It is for the sake of the led. It is a proper altruism."[59]

It has been observed that servant leadership is somewhat similar to transformational leadership; however, servant leadership is distinguishable because of its strong focus on the followers. Since the early 1990s there has been a continuing increase in the attention given to "servant leadership," including a dramatic rise in research conducted on service leadership and efforts to implement service leadership into organizational practice.[60] Spears, one of the most influential scholars in the area of servant leadership, offered the following list of the 10 characteristics of servant leadership[61]:

---

[58] Greenleaf, R. 1977. *Servant Leadership: A Journey into the Nature of Legitimate Power and Greatness*, 27 New York, NY: Paulist Press.

[59] Tutu, D. October 2, 2009. "Forging Equality in South Africa." *Academy of Achievement*, http://achievement.org/autodoc/printmember/tut0int-1

[60] Extensive reviews of the literature and research surrounding servant leadership can be found in McIntosh, T.A., J.A. Irving, and B. Seminary. 2008. "Evaluating the Instrumento de Contribución al Liderazgo de Siervo (ICLS) for Reliability in Latin America." *Journal of Virtues and Leadership* 1, no. 1, pp. 30–49; and Molnar, D. 2007. *Serving the World: A Cross-Cultural study of National Culture Dimensions and Servant Leadership* [Dissertation] *Abstracts International* 68, no. (5–A), p. 2052. UMI No. AAI3266277. Molnar's dissertation provides an interesting international comparison of the relationship between culture and servant leadership. See also Blanchard, K., and R. Broadwell. 2018. *Servant Leadership in Action: How You Can Achieve Great Relationships and Results*. Oakland, CA: Berrett-Koehler Publishers.

[61] Spears, L. 2004. "The Understanding and Practice of Servant-Leadership." In *Practicing Servant Leadership: Succeeding through Trust, Bravery, and Forgiveness*, eds. L. Spears and M. Lawrence, 9–24. San Francisco: Jossey-Bass.

1. Listening: Listening, coupled with regular periods of reflection, is essential to the growth of the servant-leader.
2. Empathy: The servant-leader strives to understand and empathize with others.
3. Healing: Learning to heal is a powerful force for transformation and integration.
4. Awareness: General awareness, and especially self-awareness, strengthens the servant-leader.
5. Persuasion: The servant-leader seeks to persuade others rather than to coerce compliance.
6. Conceptualization: The ability to look at a problem (or an organization) from a conceptualizing perspective means that one must think beyond day-to-day realities.
7. Foresight: Foresight is a characteristic that enables the servant-leader to understand the lessons from the past, the realities of the present, and the likely consequences of a decision for the future.
8. Stewardship: Servant-leadership, like stewardship, assumes first and foremost a commitment to serving the needs of others.
9. Commitment to the growth of people: Servant-leaders believe that people have an intrinsic value beyond their tangible contributions as workers.
10. Building community: Servant-leadership suggests that true community can be created among those who work in businesses and other institutions.

Russell and Stone reviewed the leadership on servant literature to create a list of the "functional attributes" of servant leaders, which they explained were the "operative qualities, characteristics, and distinctive features belonging to leaders and observed through specific leader behaviors in the workplace."[62] This list included vision, honesty, integrity, trust, service, modeling, pioneering, appreciation of others, empowerment, teaching, and delegation. In addition, Russell and Stone offered

---

[62] Russell, R., and A. Stone. 2002. "A Review of Servant Leadership Attributes: Developing a Practical Model." *Leadership and Organization Development Journal* 23, no. 3, pp. 145–57, 146.

the following list of "accompanying attributes," which they explained to be secondary characteristics which complement the functional list: communication, credibility, competence, stewardship, visibility, influence, persuasion, listening, and encouragement. Patterson's attempt to develop a model of servant leadership included presentation of the following "component constructs underlying the practice of servant leadership": "Agapao Love," which means to love in a social or moral sense; humility, the ability to keep one's accomplishments and successes in perspective; altruism, which means helping others selflessly just for the sake of helping; vision, which was cited as being necessary for good leadership; trust, which speaks to leader morality and competence; service, which was defined as a mission of responsibility to others; and, finally, empowerment by entrusting power to others.[63]

Coach Dean Smith as a Servant Leader

An interesting and entertainment perspective on the practice of servant leadership comes from an article published online on the Championship Coaches Network soon after the death of Dean Smith, the legendary long-time basketball coach at the University of North Carolina who collaborated with Dr. Jerry Bell to write and publish a book, "The Carolina Way," that included many of Smith's ideas for effective coaching and leadership. The article used quotes from the book to illustrate "10 Leadership Lessons from Coach Dean Smith" and the author observed that "Coach Smith was practicing servant leadership long before it has become the popular management principle it is today." In fact, the following quotes from the book are quite clear on how Smith approached his relationship with his players: "The coach's job is to be part servant in helping each player reach his goals within the team concept" (p. 147) and

> When I became head coach at North Carolina, I tried to put myself in the shoes of the players. How did they want to be

---

[63] Patterson, K.A. 2003. *Servant Leadership: A Theoretical Model* [Doctoral Dissertation] *Abstracts International*, 64, no. 2, p. 570, UMI No. 3082719.

treated? How could I help them reach their potential? How could I make the game fun and enjoyable and still work them hard? (p. 200)

Other key characteristics of servant leadership highlighted in the article using quotes from the book included the following:

- **Genuine caring for followers**: "The most important thing in good leadership is truly caring. The best leaders in any profession care about the people they lead, and the people who are being led know when the caring is genuine and when it's faked or not there at all" (p. 4). Smith was famous for building and maintaining long-term relationships with all of his players that extended far past the day that a player's eligibility ended.
- **Willingness and ability to earn commitment of followers**: "A leader's job is to develop committed followers. Bad leaders destroy their followers' sense of commitment" (p. 33). Smith argued that leaders can no longer demand or expect automatic respect from their followers and must be prepared to earn commitment, respect, and trust from followers, a process that requires leaders to act with integrity and credibility.
- **Confidence building**: "I'd get on the players if I needed to, but it was also important to praise them for the good things they had done, especially on the road, where they faced enough adversity without my piling on. I wasn't as critical during games as I was at practice. Players needed confidence during games more than criticism" (p. 240). Whereas constructive criticism is necessary for skill building and correcting errors that are undermining performance, leaders should be sensitive to how and when feedback that is likely to be perceived as negative is delivered.
- **Team building**: In the book Bell explained Smith's approach to team building as follows: "Part of Dean

Smith's greatness as a leader lies in his ability to get his players to get beyond understanding their roles to embracing them. But their commitment starts with clarity. If employees don't understand their roles, their specific areas of responsibility, it's almost impossible for the company to work well as a team. Confusion will reign. Divided responsibility ends up being nobody's responsibility" (p. 137). The article emphasized the need for leaders to invest time and effort with every employee, not just the "stars," to set and define their roles within the organization, explain how they are contributing to the organization, and establish a plan for them to follow in order to expand and change their roles as time goes by.

The other principles of leadership highlighted in the article, although not as directly related to servant leadership as those previously outlined, were nonetheless complimentary and flowed naturally from Smith's fundamental approach to relating to his players. For example, "fair and consistent" punishment was mentioned as an element of team building and inconsistent punishment will almost certainly undermine a leader's attempt to establish and maintain commitment from followers. In addition, by caring for players from the moment they entered the program and continuously working with them to defining their roles and build confidence Smith was able to develop a group of senior leaders who could mentor younger players and tell them what was expected of them and what it would take to achieve their goals. Smith also made the process of confidence building easier and clearer by creating a daily "emphasis" and "thought," based on Smith's core principles and philosophies, which became the focal points of teaching and reinforcement during practices. Finally, Smith built credibility among his players by demonstrating through his words and actions that although team performance, and winning, was very important and certainly a source of pressure for everyone involved, his priorities with respect to his players were not grounded in results on the court but on helping them to get a good education and become good citizens.

Source: "10 Leadership Lessons from Coach Dean Smith." Championship Coaches Network (blog), http://championshipcoachesnetwork.com/public/315.cfm (accessed December 14, 2018). See also Smith, D., and G. Bell. 2004. *The Carolina Way: Leadership Lessons from a Life in Coaching.* New York, NY: The Penguin Press.

Silicon Valley Leadership Styles

Academics exploring leadership of emerging companies in the United States have suggested a variety of frameworks for classifying and explaining "leadership styles" Inc. focused on four strategies—directive, participative, laissez-faire, and adaptive—and suggested that the dynamic environment in which emerging companies operated required that leaders be able to apply each of the styles at the appropriate moment.[64] A PsychTests study of more than 7,000 top-performing leaders, including leaders of firms other than emerging companies, confirmed the advice from Inc. by finding that the most effective leadership style in terms of firm performance could best be described as "eclectic" and incorporated elements of four other distinct leadership styles identified in that same study: the "sports coach," the driver-director, the mentor, and the "country clubber."[65]

An article in Fast Company described the menu of leadership styles developed by Goleman in his 2000 study of mid-level managers: pacesetting, authoritative, affiliative, coaching, coercive, and democratic.[66] Obviously the apparent ability to identify and describe a particular leadership style does not mean that it is effective or used as often as it should be. For example, Goleman found that his pacesetting and coercive styles typically produced a negative impact on leadership effectiveness and that his coaching style, which he argued could be quite effective, was often

---

[64] Blickenstaff, G. 2012. *4 Leadership Styles to Master.*

[65] Kay, A. June 29, 2013. *At Work: One Size Doesn't Fit All on Leadership.*

[66] Benincasa, R. 2012. *6 Leadership Styles and When You Should Use Them.* (citing Goleman, D. March-April 2000. "Leadership That Gets Results." *Harvard Business Review* 78, no. 2, pp. 4–17.)

kept on the shelf by leaders who feared it would take too long to apply.[67] Complicating the area even further is that argument of researchers such as Kets de Vries that companies can no longer look to a single omnipresent ruler but must instead recognize that success is tied to creating and maintaining a team of self-aware executives that learn how to work together to apply "distributive, collective, and complementary leadership."[68] Kets de Vries suggested that the "leadership team" have the capability to carry out eight different archetypical roles including strategist, change-catalyst, transactor, building, innovator, processor, coach, and communicator.[69]

The extraordinary financial and inventive success of Apple, and the death of its iconic leader Steve Jobs, has served as a platform for a robust debate about whether or not Jobs should be lauded for his leadership practices and style. Williams, writing for Psychology Today, noted that many management consultants, academics, and business leaders had applauded Job for his work as a "leader" and pointed to research conducted among the heads of Silicon Valley companies that showed meaningful support for Jobs' often abusive behavior as necessary for building a financially successful company (i.e., the "ends justifies the means").[70] Williams, who described Jobs' leadership style as autocratic, egotistical, and lacking in transparency and generally based on an old-style "carrot and stick" approach, suggested that "claiming Steve Jobs was a great leader smacks more of hero worship than an objective view of what a great organizational leader should be and do" and warned that "extolling his virtues to a new generation of up-and-coming leaders would be a serious mistake."[71] He also pointed to research arguing that, Apple

---

[67] Id.

[68] Yakowicz, W. 2013. *Leadership: 8 Archetypes Explained.* Inc. (citing De Vries, M.F.K. 2011. *The Hedgehog Effect: The Secrets of Building High Performance Teams.* John Wiley & Sons.)

[69] Kets de Vries, M.F.R. 2013. "The Eight Archetypes of Leadership." *Harvard Business Review.*

[70] Williams, R. April 7, 2012. "Why Steve Jobs Was Not a Leader." *Psychology Today.* (citing Sutton, R.I. 2007. *The No-Asshole Rule: Building a Civilized Workplace Surviving One That Isn't.* UK: Hachette.)

[71] Id.

notwithstanding, an abusive leadership style is not the road to optimal sustainable bottom-line performance.

Other well-known Silicon Valley-based companies have also generated commentary regarding the leadership styles that have been used to build their organizations. Thompson has written that Google has attempted to avoid excessive oversight of employees and provide them with substantial leeway, and resources, to develop new ideas that they might think of on their own.[72] Critics have scoffed at the efficacy of this approach from a financial perspective, arguing that most of the new products that have been developed have not been successful; however, it appears that the system has produced important intangible benefits in the form of a work-force that feels "personally invested in the company's sense of mission and future success."[73] According to Manimala and Wasdani the five key precepts of the leadership practices of Eric Schmidt, Google's chief executive officer, were

> get to know your employees, create new ways to reward and promote your high-performing employees, let your employees own the problems you want them to solve, allow employees to function outside the company hierarchy, and have your employees' performance reviewed by someone they respect for their objectivity and impartiality.[74]

Manimala and Wasdani also reported that an internal Google research team headed by the Laszlo Bock, Google's senior executive for human resources, had identified the following eight qualities among the best and most-effective leader-managers within the company:

> be a good coach, empower your team and don't micromanage, express interest in your team members' success and well-being, be productive and results-oriented, be a good communicator and

---

[72] Thompson, S. Google's Business Leadership and Organizational Culture.
[73] Id.
[74] Manimala, M., and K. Wasdani. May/June 2013. "Distributed Leadership at Google: Lessons from the Billion-Dollar." *Brand, Ivey Business Journal.*

listen to your team, help your employees with career development, have a clear vision and strategy for the team … [and] … have technical skills so you can advise the team.[75]

Sustainable Leadership

Although all leaders should have a vision and desire to inspire their followers to take collective action to make it happen, sustainability leaders can be distinguished as people who inspire and support action to identify and develop innovative sustainable solutions, business models, and practices that will lead to a better world. Sustainable leadership focuses on bringing about dramatic changes and requires taking a long-term perspective in making decisions; fostering systemic innovation aimed at increasing customer value; developing a skilled, loyal, and highly engaged workforce; offering quality products, services, and solutions; and engaging in ethical behavior and decision-making, and establishing ethical values and standards throughout the organization. In order to be effective, sustainability leaders must develop and practice several important habits including a systemic, interdisciplinary understanding; emotional intelligence and a caring attitude; values orientation that shapes culture; a strong vision for making a difference; an inclusive style that engenders trust; a willingness to innovate and be radical; and a long-term perspective on impacts. In addition, they must implement a number of initiatives to establish and maintain the foundation for sustainability throughout their organizations including training and staff development programs, proactively striving for amicable labor relations, development of strategies for staff retention, shifting compensation programs toward metrics that valued contributions to customer loyalty and to innovation, promoting environmental and social responsibility, initiating communications with multiple stakeholders and transparently taking into account and balancing their interests, and developing and embedding a share vision for the goals of the business.

There is a considerable body of evidence that shows that sustainable leadership practices are more likely to enhance business performance over

---

[75] Id.

the long term than the traditional approach that puts the interests of shareholders first and focuses primarily on short-term financial metrics. Done well, sustainable leadership leads to several desirable performance outcomes including integrity of brand and reputation, enhanced customer satisfaction, solid operational finances that ensure viability and organizational sustainability and provide capital for investment in innovation, and long-term value for multiple stakeholders.

Visser and Courtice suggested that "a sustainability leader is someone who inspires and supports action toward a better world."[76] They also noted that the Sustainability Leadership Institute (www.sustainabilityleadershipinstitute.org) had identified sustainability leaders as "individuals who are compelled to make a difference by deepening their awareness of themselves in relation to the world around them. In doing so, they adopt new ways of seeing, thinking and interacting that result in innovative, sustainable solutions." Visser and Courtice argued that "leadership for sustainability" should not be treated as a separate school of leadership but rather should be viewed in a manner akin to the contingency/interaction school: a particular blend of leadership characteristics applied within a specific context (i.e., the sustainability challenges facing the world and the aspirations of multiple stakeholders for a more sustainable future). They suggested that whereas it may currently be necessary to differentiate sustainability leadership from leadership in general, the distinction may erode as time goes by and sustainability becomes more embedded in organizations in much the same way as the focus on quality did in the 1980s and 1990s.

Avery and Bergsteiner argued that there is a considerable body of evidence that shows that sustainable leadership practices are more likely to enhance business performance over the long term than the traditional approach that puts the interests of shareholders first and focuses primarily on short-term financial metrics.[77] For example, companies that take

---

[76] Visser, W., and P. Courtice. 2011. *Sustainability Leadership: Linking Theory and Practice*, 2. Cambridge UK, University of Cambridge Institute for Sustainability Leadership.

[77] Id. at p. 11 (citing Ghoshal, S. 2005. "Bad Management Theories are Destroying Good Management Practices." *Academy of Management Learning & Education* 4, no. 1, p. 75).

a long-term perspective, and attract patient investors that share sustainability values, are able to reap benefits from investing in their people, innovative technologies, and strong and enduring relationships with customers and suppliers. This allows those companies to build trust, accumulate and retain knowledge by working hard to train employees and retain them through development programs and finding ways to keep them during difficult economic times, and build an organizational culture that is readily adaptable to change and new opportunities. Moreover, savings realized from recycling and improving the eco-efficiency of operational activities not only strengthens financial performance but can also be re-invested in other environmental and social initiatives.[78] Companies also find that many of the practices associated with sustainable leadership, such as focusing on staff retention and development, ultimately turn out to be important sources of competitive advantage.[79]

In spite of the advantages to practicing sustainable leadership, old practices are often hard to discard and the changes associated with shifting toward sustainability are often risky and disruptive and carry both financial and intangible costs. Avery and Bergsteiner also pointed out that

---

[78] Avery and Bergsteiner suggested that sustainably led organizations had been identified across different sectors, countries, institutional contexts, and markets and included unlisted companies such as WL Gore & Associates (Goretexw and other products) and SAS (software) in the United States; Giesecke & Devrient (bank notes and securities) and Kärcher (cleaning solutions) in Germany; and Endress & Hauser (flow technologies) and Migros (retail conglomerate) in Switzerland. Id. at p. 10.

[79] Id. at p. 12 (citing Ichniowski, C., K. Shaw, and G. Prennushi. 1999. "The Effects of Human Resource Management Practices on Productivity: A Study of Steel Finishing Lines." *American Economic Review* 87, no. 3, p. 291); Pfau, B., and S. Cohen. 2003. "Aligning Human Capital Practices and Employee Behavior with Shareholder Value." *Consulting Psychology Journal* 55, no. 3, p. 169; Cascio, W. 2002. *Responsible Restructuring: Creative and Profitable Alternatives to Layoffs.* San Francisco, CA: Berrett-Koehler; D'Souza, R., L. Strazdins, M. Clements, D. Broom, R. Parslow, and B. Rodgers. 2005. "The Health Effects of Jobs: Status, Working Conditions, or Both?" *Australian & New Zealand Journal of Public Health* 29, no. 3, p. 222; Pfau, B., and S. Cohen. 2003. "Aligning Human Capital Practices and Employee Behavior with Shareholder Value." *Consulting Psychology Journal* 55, no. 3, p. 169.

sustainable leadership systems are vulnerable to a variety of external events such as mergers and acquisitions, which bring in new employees, customers, suppliers, and other stakeholders who may not share the core values of sustainability that had been developed prior to the transaction; taking on additional major shareholders who may have different ideas about what constitutes acceptable performance for the business; or the hiring of new executives who are not familiar with the organizational cultures and may bring different values from their prior positions.[80] Downturns in financial and consumer markets will also put a strain on sustainable leadership practices as companies must address economic survival and make hard decisions about laying off employees and cutting back investments in training and development and innovation aimed at protecting the environment and social responsibility. Although sustainable leaders realize that they live and operate in a world in which short-term results still matter, they also know that violating ethical principles to appease investors or ignoring the interests of nonfinancial stakeholders can significantly and permanently damage their organizational culture and undermine their long-term goals and success.[81]

---

[80] Avery, G., and H. Bergsteiner. 2011. "Sustainable Leadership Practices for Enhancing Business Resilience and Performance." *Strategy and Leadership* 39, no. 3, pp. 5–10.

[81] Avery and Bergsteiner conceded that it was likely to be more difficult for listed corporations or private equity groups to operate on sustainable principles because of the pressures on them to achieve short-term performance goals; however, they identified several listed companies that had successfully managed their relationships with financial markets while simultaneously operating in a sustainable manner: Munich Re (finance) in Germany; Colgate (consumer goods) in the United States; BT Group (telecommunications) in the United Kingdom; Siam Cement Group (construction) in Thailand; and Holcim (construction) in Switzerland. Id. at p. 10.

CHAPTER 5

Leadership in Developing Countries

Introduction

The field of "leadership studies" has long been primarily focused on western leadership styles and practices.[1] This occurred for various reasons including the location of the critical mass of researchers in the United States and the fact that most companies operated primarily in the United States with some cautious expansion into foreign markets with similar linguistic and cultural traditions. However, several factors—globalization of the workforce, expansion of operations into numerous countries and regions around the world, and exposure to increase global competition—has forced leadership scholars to incorporate culture into their research and theories because leaders of businesses of all sizes in all countries must be prepared to interact with customers and other business partners from different cultures and leaders of larger companies have the additional challenge of managing multinational organizations and aligning a global corporate culture with multiple and diverging national cultures. In addition, there has been a growing recognition that the study of leadership in developing countries, and training of prospective leaders in those countries, is important because leaders in developing countries can, "by creating vision, direction and collective purposes," play a pivotal role in

---

[1] For a general introduction to the area of leadership studies including definitional concepts and a history of the evolution of leadership studies, see "History and Evolution of Leadership Studies" prepared and distributed by the Sustainable Entrepreneurship Project (www.seproject.org).

resolving multiple collection action problems that impede social development and economic growth in those countries.[2]

It is now well accepted that leadership "matters" when it comes to economic growth and development, a conclusion that follows the previous realization that institutions are important contributors to the social and economic progress of developing countries. However, scholars such as de Ver have been critical of research efforts relating to leadership in developing countries, arguing that "many of the conceptions of leadership in the literature are Western-oriented, universalist or individualistic, and there are few conceptions which either incorporate a political understanding of leadership as a process or which have developmental salience."[3] She has also expressed a concern that little analysis has been conducted on how leadership can be practiced in what she describes as "the very often unstable, hybrid and evolving institutional contexts which characterize the condition of many developing countries." She counseled that leadership needed to be understood as a political process, particularly in developing countries, and leadership occurred "within a given indigenous configuration of power, authority and legitimacy, shaped by history, institutions, goals and political culture." She noted that in developing countries, leaders must be able to forge formal or informal coalitions, vertical or horizontal, to solve collective action problems and that the influence of informal institutions is much greater in developing countries and it was thus imperative for leaders to understand those institutions and engage with them in order to be effective.

After conducting an extensive survey of the general literature on "leadership," de Ver concluded that relatively little work had been done on leadership in the specific context of developing countries and the unique problems that the social, economic, and political environments in those countries create for their prospective leaders. Her specific findings included the following[4]:

---

[2] de Ver, H.L. April 2008. *Leadership, Politics and Development: A Literature Survey.* (Development Leadership Program, Background Paper.) www.dlprog. org/ftp/.../Leadership,%20Politics%20and%20Development.pdf, 4

[3] Id.

[4] Id. at pp. 3–6.

- Leadership as concept and practice has neither been properly researched nor understood analytically as a key element in the politics of economic growth and social development, and the available literature seldom addresses those key issues.
- The bulk of the literature focuses on individuals and individual capacities, or attributes (i.e., individual leaders' characteristics, qualities, attributes, or traits), and not on leadership as a political process involving both leaders' relations with followers and, more critically, elites and coalitions and their interactions.
- Much of the general leadership literature has a distinctly western, business-related focus with a particular emphasis on leadership from a managerial and organizational perspective. This is not surprising given that most of the scholars working in the field of "leadership studies" are based in the United States and many of the leading textbooks on the subject have generally included few case studies and examples set in the developing world while focusing most of the attention on western management systems.
- Only a small body of "mainstream leadership literature" addresses the role of leadership for economic and social development and what is available is largely confined to empirical studies of individual cases.
- What literature there is on leadership in developing countries pays little attention to issues concerning leaders, elites, and coalitions.
- There are substantial policy-relevant research gaps to be filled. For example, de Ver urges the research community to move toward creating and expanding a library of case studies that illustrate the role that leaders, elites, and coalitions in developing countries have played in successfully achieving sustained economic growth, social development, and organizational success. Cases studies should focus on national, subnational, sectorial, and organizational activities.

Although de Ver's critiques are varied and diverse, she correctly points out the problems that arise when so much of the leadership-related research is based on an assumption of universal acceptance of western business culture, which she describes as one "in which profit is the main indicator of success and the main goal."[5] The following passage illustrates how and why application of a western "cultural hegemony" can lead to puzzling and problematic results in developing countries:

[In the West there is] the belief that people are rational actors, that markets should be given predominance over the state, and that individualism and competition have inherent merits. In other cultures, however, these assumptions are not universally accepted and often the opposite is the case. For example . . . in much of East Asia emphasis is placed on conformity, notions of interpersonal harmony and collectivism or group-centeredness. This is in clear contrast to the Western functionalist paradigm where emphasis is placed on autonomy, competition between individuals and groups, performance and self-assertion. In Africa, a different culture of leadership, again, is visible, with emphasis on ceremony, ritual, interpersonal relations, reciprocity, and the distribution of scant resources to clan and ethnic affiliates over and above profit and competition.[6]

Another problem with relying on western-based notions of organizational and managerial leadership for analyzing developing countries is the implicit assumption that the political environment and business systems are relatively stable. In fact, formal rules, regulations, and accepted practices are often unavailable, or ignored, in developing countries. Although the situation is slowly changing as developing countries engage in wholesale restructuring and strengthening of their institutions, it is still generally the case that leaders in developing countries must operate in an environment in which rules change constantly and change is accepted slowly and often with great suspicion by followers. This is one of the

---

[5] Id.

[6] Id. at p. 16 (based on omitted quotes from and citations to Blunt, P., and M. Jones. 1997. "Exploring the Limits of Western Leadership Theory in East Asia and Africa." *Personnel Review* 26, nos. 1/2, pp. 6–23).

reasons that a key role of an organizational leader in a developing country is protecting the organization against the possibility of adverse changes in policy by public institutions, because the state continues to exercise substantial influence in the marketplaces of developing countries.

Culture and Leadership in Developing Countries

As in all countries, leaders in developing countries act within a specific sociocultural environment and the characteristics of that environment are presumed to be important determinants of the efficacy of the leader's style and practices. Aycan suggested a profile of the "typical" cultural environment in developing countries that included a strong emphasis on relationships and networking; a strong family orientation that impacts both the personal and work lives of society members; low individual performance orientation, consistent with the strong relationship orientation and collectivist nature of most developing country societies; a low sense of control and self-efficacy, leading to a feeling of "fatalism" and a sense that events are out of the control of society members; downward, indirect, and nonconfrontational communication patterns; and, finally, a strong authority orientation rooted in respect, loyalty, and deference toward those in positions of authority.[7] She also cautioned, however, that there will certainly be significant cultural differences among the large number of countries still classified as "developing" and that within each country one will find differences among individuals—because of education, socioeconomic status, or age; regional and ethic subcultures; and business organizations (e.g., subsidiaries of multinational corporations will likely have different cultural orientations than indigenous family-owned businesses).

Using societal culture as a reference point, Pasa et al. provided a suggested list of the expectations and assumptions of leaders in developing countries with respect to their followers along with a profile of leader preferences regarding their own styles and behavior. Specifically, they

---

[7] Aycan, Z. 2004. "Leadership and Teamwork in Developing Countries: Challenges and Opportunities." In *Online Readings in Psychology and Culture*, eds. W. Lonner, D. Dinnel, S. Hayes, and D. Sattler.

argued that in developing countries leaders "are more likely to assume that their employees have an external locus of control, have limited and fixed potential, operate from a time perspective that is past and present oriented and have a short-time focus."[8] With respect to the actual behavior of leaders in developing countries, Pasa et al. predicted that they "are more likely to encourage a passive or reactive stance to task performance, judge success on moralism derived from tradition and religion, favour an authoritarian or paternalistic orientation and accept that consideration of the context overrides principles and rules."[9] Jaeger observed that

> [t]he relatively high power distance and the authoritarian/paternalistic people orientation of developing countries imply a certain type of leadership behaviour and leader–follower relationship . . . characterized as being more congruent with "Theory X" leadership, which . . . presupposes limited and fixed human potential.

It is certainly problematic and dangerous to make generalizations regarding the elements of societal culture that can be found in the large swath of countries around the world that are classified as "developing." However, cultural profiles developed by researchers may be used as a means for creating hypotheses about the issues and problems that will likely confront leaders in developing countries and the solutions that might be used in order to motivate followers to act in ways that contribute to the achievement of goals established for the organization. In addition, understanding the cultural profile of the country in which a leader is operating provides a clue regarding the preferred personality traits and work values of leaders; the manner in which leaders should seek to relate to their subordinates, including the degree to which leaders are expected to be involved in the personal affairs of subordinates and their families;

---

[8] Pasa, S., H. Kabasakal, and M. Bodur. 2001. "Society, Organisations and Leadership in Turkey." *Applied Psychology: An International Review* 50, no. 4, pp. 559–89, 563. (citing Kanungo, R., and A. Jaeger. 1990. "Introduction: The Need for Indigenous Management in Developing Countries." In *Management in Developing Countries*, eds. A. Jaeger and R. Kanungo. London: Routledge.)

[9] Id. at p. 563.

the basis upon which a leader can attain "legitimacy" in the eyes of those that he or she is seeking to leader; and, finally, the effectiveness of particular leadership styles and behaviors.[10]

Relationship Orientation and Paternalism

The strong relationship orientation found in many developing countries explains the popularity and prevalence of the paternalistic leadership style in developing countries. Leaders, like others in those countries, place great importance on establishing and maintaining interpersonal relationships with others including subordinates in the workplace. In turn, subordinates also expect a relationship with their superior that is personal yet professional and characterized by protection, close guidance, and supervision. In exchange for the responsibilities that leaders take for their lives, subordinates are loyal and deferential to their leaders and are generally willing to follow their directions without question or criticism. The paternalistic relationship between leaders and subordinates in developing countries is analogous to a parent–child relationship and, as is the case in the familial context, the relationship is hierarchical with the leader assumed to "know better" for the subordinates in all areas of their lives: personal, professional, and family-related matters.[11]

Aycan argues that the evidence of paternalism can be found in numerous acts by both leaders and subordinates within and outside the workplace. For example, Aycan explains that

[t]he paternalistic leader gives advice (often times unsolicited) and guides employees in personal, professional (e.g., make career

---

[10] Jaeger, A. 1990. "The Applicability of Western Management Techniques in Developing Countries: A Cultural Perspective." In *Management in Developing Countries*, eds. A. Jaeger and R. Kanungo, 131–45, 263, 139. London: Routledge. For further discussion of "Theory X" leadership, see "Human Resources: A Library of Resources for Sustainable Entrepreneurs" prepared and distributed by the Sustainable Entrepreneurship Project (www.seproject.org).

[11] Aycan, Z. 2004. "Leadership and Teamwork in Developing Countries: Challenges and Opportunities." In *Online Readings in Psychology and Culture*, eds. W. Lonner, D. Dinnel, S. Hayes, and D. Sattler.

planning on their behalf), and family-related matters (e.g., do marriage counseling, resolve disputes between husband and wives, etc.); shows concern for the well-being of the subordinate as well as his/her family; attends congratulatory (e.g., weddings) and condolence (e.g., funerals) ceremonies of employees as well as their immediate family members; when in need, provides financial assistance to employees (in form of donations or sometimes as loans) in, for example, housing, health care, and educational expenses of their children; allows them to attend personal or family-related problems by letting them leave early or take a day off; acts as a mediator in interpersonal conflicts among employees, and even talks to the disputed party on behalf of the other (without his knowledge or consent) to resolve the conflict.[12]

In return, subordinates are willing to go to great lengths to demonstrate their loyalty and deference to their leaders including

engaging in extra-role behavior or working overtime (unpaid) upon the request of the supervisor; not quitting the job (even if one receives a much better job offer) because of loyalty; following the paternalistic superior to another organization if s/he quits the company; not questioning nor disagreeing with the superior in decisions regarding the company or the employee (e.g., performance evaluations, career-planning, etc.); doing personal favors for the superior when needed (e.g., helping him during the construction of his house); putting extra effort in the job and working hard, so not to lose face to the superior.[13]

Family Orientation

Family orientation is an important influence on societal culture in developing countries and plays an important part in how subordinates view work activities in the larger context of their lives and how subordinates

---

[12] Id.
[13] Id.

expect their leaders to act in an organizational context. In most cases, subordinates view work primarily as a means for satisfying the needs of their families and advancing the family's status within society. In addition, subordinates expect that the organizations they work for will take care of them and their families and it is common to find organizations offering health and educational services to their workers and their families, contributing to housing and heating expenses, and providing financial assistance to workers who may be experiencing problems. Family obligations are routinely allowed to take precedence over work. Aycan explained that "employees feel entitled to absent themselves from work for family-related reasons . . . [w]ork always comes next to family, and there is nothing more natural than this."[14] Family orientation is also expressed through the preference for subordinate–superior relationships in the workplace that are analogous to the way that a parent (i.e., the superior) interacts with a child (i.e., the subordinate) and vice versa.

Harmony and Individual Performance Orientation

One of the most vexing issues for leaders steeped in Anglo-style values and practices is establishing reward systems in developing countries that are intended to motivate subordinates to establish and pursue individual goals and objectives. The importance placed on maintaining good and harmonious interpersonal relationships tends to stifle individual performance orientation in developing countries. Subordinates are expected to concentrate on loyalty and compliance toward their superiors and acting in ways that promote, rather than disturb, harmony with their coworkers. This means that any action that causes a person to "stand out" within his or her group is frowned upon and may lead to jealousy and isolation of that person. In turn, persons who are having trouble fulfilling their quotas or otherwise keeping up with others will usually be tolerated and treated with compassion as long as they are doing their best and have an honest intention to contribute to the work of the group.[15] Muczyk and

---

[14] Id.

[15] For further discussion, see Kabasakal, H., and A. Dastmalchian. 2001. "Leadership and Culture in the Middle East." *Applied Psychology: An International Review* 50, no. 4, pp. 559–89.

Holt noted that in light of the collectivist nature of many societies classified as "developing" it is not surprising that group and/or organizational measures of performance are recommended as the basis for rewards.[16]

Low Sense of Control and Self-Efficacy

The low levels of sense of control and self-efficacy often found in developing countries causes persons to believe that events are based primarily on external causes outside of their control or influence. As a result, many people in developing countries look at activities such as planning, scheduling, and goal setting as being pointless. They are also reluctant to be proactive and take initiative because they feel that there is little likelihood that such an approach will make a difference, given that results are out of their control, and there are concerns that individual initiative will simply increase risks and uncertainty and that challenging the status quo will disrupt harmony within the group. Poor or mediocre behavior may be explained, and tolerated, in developing countries as simply being a person's "destiny."

Communication Patterns

Aycan noted that organizational communication patterns in developing countries tend to be "indirect, non-assertive, non-confrontational, and usually downwards,"[17] which is consistent with the hierarchical nature of organizations and the acceptance of authority from and at the top of the hierarchy. This has a number of consequences for organizational leaders in developing countries. First, honest and complete performance evaluations are extremely difficult because negative feedback, even when intended to improve performance, is seen as when Aycan described as "destructive

---

[16] Muczyk, J., and D. Holt. May 2008. "Toward a Cultural Contingency Model of Leadership." *Journal of Leadership & Organizational Studies* 14, no. 4, pp. 277–86, 283.

[17] Aycan, Z. 2004. "Leadership and Teamwork in Developing Countries: Challenges and Opportunities." In *Online Readings in Psychology and Culture*, eds. W. Lonner, D. Dinnel, S. Hayes, and D. Sattler.

criticism" and often misconstrued as being a personal attack on the recipient. Feedback, when given, must also be presented in a way that does not cause the recipient to lose "face" among his or her peers and in the eyes of his or her superiors. Finally, negative feedback may be viewed as disrupting the all-important sense of harmony within the group. Second, downward communication patterns mean that little, if any, feedback flows from subordinates up to their superiors. This is not surprising given the deference shown to those in positions of authority; however, the lack of information from lower levels of the organization may undermine the leader's ability to make appropriate decisions and make adjustments to directions that have already been issued. Aycan also noted that "[t]here is strong preference for face-to-face communication in business dealings" in developing countries.[18] Although this type of communication should, presumably, reduce the risk of misunderstanding it also tends to be more time consuming and may lead to delays in completing specific tasks and entire projects.

Leader Authority and Power

The almost absolute authority of superiors in an organizational context in developing countries is consistent with the authority orientation that permeates societal culture in those countries. Superiors are entitled to, and receive, respect, loyalty, and deference and are trusted because of their knowledge, experience, and achievements. Although organizational rules may be prescribed, subordinates act based on their respect for authority rather than because they are expected to follow rules and procedures. Subordinates rarely challenge those in authority and accept that although superiors are part of the "in-group" they have a higher status that separates them from other group members and entitles them to certain privileges and advantages. Superiors in developing countries often have close relationships with their subordinates, including close and extensive participation in the personal lives of subordinates; however, these relationships are not to be confused with "friendship" and typically remain formal and distant.

---

[18] Id.

The respect for, and acceptance of, a leader's authority in developing countries is accompanied by a strong desire among leaders to exercise the power they have been given over their subordinates and their firms. Ideally, at least from the perspective of the subordinates, power will be exercise in a manner that is consistent with good interpersonal relations between leaders and their subordinates—a style that Aycan describes as "benevolent paternalism,"[19] which is characterized by a leader exercising his or her power for the benefit of subordinates in the same way that a parent directs and disciplines his or her children for "their own good." Often, however, leaders in developing countries engage in what Aycan called "exploitative paternalism" and use their power and status for their personal benefit and the advantage of their families and other in-group members.[20] Even when leaders engage in benevolent paternalism they still insist in various manifestations of their power and authority such as formality and respect in personal relationships with subordinates. In addition, the inequality of power between leaders and subordinates leads to centralization and unilateral decision-making by the leader. Consultation with subordinates is rare, even nonexistent, because leaders believe that encouraging participation in decision-making by subordinates will undermine their power and make them look weak. For their part, subordinates in developing countries are generally tolerant of apparently dictatorial practices of their leaders with respect to decisions and instructions because they trust the wisdom and competencies of the leader and are themselves reluctant to take on the risks and responsibilities that come with making decisions.

Leader Networking Responsibilities

The importance of relationships between leaders and their subordinates in developing countries has already been discussed earlier; however, the relationship orientation typically found in those countries extends outside of the workplace in the form of the extensive efforts that leaders in developing countries must make in order to establish and maintain good

---

[19] Id.
[20] Id.

relations with those in positions of power within key institutions such as the government. The scarcity of technical and financial resources in developing countries, and the role that local politics plays in who controls those resources and how they are allocated, means that organizational leaders in those countries must proactively seek to protect the interests of their firms. Accordingly, Aycan notes that developing countries leaders must be skilled in "networking and diplomacy."[21]

Effective Leadership Practices for Developing Countries

Whereas research on the influence of societal culture on leadership is not as prevalent with respect to developing countries as it is with western societies, anecdotal evidence appears to provide support for the proposition that the actions of leaders in developing countries are significantly influenced by cultural factors. Aycan succinctly summarized and described the key opportunities and challenges confronting leaders operating in developing countries in the following manner:

> Loyalty, trust and affection for the leader; importance of harmonious interpersonal relationships; desire to learn and motivation to develop; self-sacrifice for the well-being of the "in-group"; flexibility. These are workforce characteristics that have great potential to enhance organizational performance, if utilized effectively. On the other hand, the global leader will be challenged to gain acceptance as an in-group member, motivate employees for higher performance, improve communication effectiveness, overcome the sense of insecurity, helplessness and dependency proneness, and administer participative decision-making.[22]

---

[21] Id.

[22] Aycan, Z. 2004. "Leadership and Teamwork in Developing Countries: Challenges and Opportunities" In *Online Readings in Psychology and Culture*, eds. W. Lonner, D. Dinnel, S. Hayes, and D. Sattler.

Although one menu of leadership styles and behaviors cannot fit every circumstance in the developing world, researchers have nonetheless attempted to suggest a universal list of the qualities of effective leadership in developing countries. For example, according to Aycan, the following characteristics should be included in an "ideal leader profile" for leaders in developing countries: empowering (able to make people feel that they are powerful); participative, but also decisive; trustworthy, knowledgeable, skillful, and administratively competent; paternalistic and also performance-oriented; fair and just, especially in interpersonal relationships; diplomatic; conscious of status differences, but at the same time modest and humble; and team integrator.[23]

Kurfi, writing with particular regard to leadership styles in Nigeria, provided the following list of "the qualities of good leadership" to which leaders in emerging economies should aspire[24]:

- A good leader serves as a personal example of good moral character and personal integrity which can and should be emulated by his or her followers.
- A good leader has competencies in the art of managing people and resources and the capacity and motivation to initiate activities and programs that are useful to his or her organization and society.
- Good leaders are able to inspire loyalty and commitment from their follower to pursue a specific vision and mission established and described by the leader.
- Good leaders are willing to subordinate their personal interests and desires and instead work to promote the interests and desires of his or her followers.
- Good leaders have clear goals and a vision of the results they want their followers to achieve and also have the capacity and knowledge to recognize and resolve problems and challenges

---

[23] Id.
[24] Kurfi, A. 2009. "Leadership Styles: The Managerial Challenges in Emerging Economies." *International Bulletin of Business Administration* 6, pp. 73–81, 79.

that are likely to be encountered on the path of pursuing those goals.

- Leaders are more likely to be effective when they are allowed to "emerge from below and not imposed from above," a concept similar to "servant-based" leadership theory.
- Effective leaders are people-oriented and should strive for empathy with the aspirations of their followers in a way that builds trust among those followers.

The qualities described by Kurfi emphasize role modeling, talents and competencies, motivation and initiative, charismatic inspiration, sacrifice, a clear sense of purpose, empathy, and participation; however, Kurfi concedes that such qualities are often lacking in developing countries such as Nigeria where leadership is frequently associated with corruption and leaders habitually neglect the welfare of the followers and the need for honor and integrity and instead concentrate on their personal interests and the interests of their own "in-group."[25] In fact, another observer of the situation in Nigeria argued that the country's main problem was the absence of the required leadership sincerity and political will to marshal the resources available to address the poverty that exists among a vast majority of the citizens of that country.[26]

The influential Global Leadership and Organizational Behaviour Effectiveness research program, or "GLOBE" study, provided evidence for the effectiveness of several different leadership profiles in country clusters in which a high proportion of the members could reasonably be

---

[25] Id. at p. 80. On the other hand, Mutabazi cautions against the popular stereotypes of corruption in Africa and argues that "corruption is no more a part of the African business mentality than it is in any other region of the world" and that embezzlement and similar crimes in Africa are "a question of personal materialism—not of African culture as a whole." Mutabazi, E. 2002. "Preparing African Leaders." In *Cross-Cultural Approaches to Leadership Development*, eds. C. Derr, S. Roussillon and F. Bournois, 202–23, 219. Westport, CN: Quorum Books.

[26] Dandago, K. 2005. "Management-Related Impediments to the Growth of the Nigerian Economy—Challenges for MBA Holders." *Journal of Social and Management Studies* (Bayero University, Kano-Nigeria) 10, 116–30, 116.

classified as "developing countries."[27] For example, the GLOBE research-ers' "charismatic/value-based" leadership style, which was universally endorsed as effective across all of the country clusters in the GLOBE study, ranked highly in the Latin American and Southern Asian clusters and even though the lowest score for this profile appeared in the Middle East cluster it was still ranked second out of the six possible styles among the respondents from that cluster. Latin Americans had the highest praise for "team-oriented" leadership among all of the country clusters and this style was also perceived quite positively by respondents from Confucian Asia and Southern Asia. Southern Asians had the strongest positive pref-erence for "humane-oriented" leadership among all of the country clus-ters in the GLOBE study and was also well regarded among respondents in the Sub-Saharan Africa and Confucian Asia clusters. Although "partici-pative" leadership was also seen as having a positive effect among develop-ing countries the enthusiasm for this style was not as great as for the other styles mentioned earlier and lagged behind the endorsements provided in the United States and other industrialized countries.

Charismatic/Value-Based Leaders

In general, charismatic/value-based leadership is well thought of all around the world regardless of which country cluster is being examined. This style of leadership is often referred to as "transformational" lead-ership, which has been defined as a leader who "engages with others in such a way that the leaders and followers raise one another to higher

---

[27] The description of the results of the GLOBE study in this paragraph is based on Javidan, M., P. Dorfman, M. de Luque, and R. House. 2006. "In the Eye of the Beholder: Cross-Cultural Lessons in Leadership from Project GLOBE." *Academy of Management Perspectives* 20, no. 1, pp. 67–90. It has been assumed that the country clusters that include a high proportion of developing countries are Latin America, Confucian Asia, Sub-Saharan Africa, Southern Asia, and the Middle East. For extensive discussion of the GLOBE study and the various lead-ership dimensions identified, defined, and assessed by the GLOBE researchers, see "Cross-Cultural Leadership Studies" prepared and distributed by the Sustain-able Entrepreneurship Project (www.seproject.org).

levels of motivation and morality."[28] Bass, one of the major proponents
of transformational leadership as a universally effective style, believed that
there are four components to transformational leadership: charisma or
idealized influence, inspirational motivation, intellectual stimulation, and
individualized consideration.[29] A number of studies appear to support the
effectiveness of transformational leadership and this style would appear to
be particularly attractive and productive in developing countries in that it
assumes that leaders are proactively engaged in creating positive changes
for their followers and the society as a whole in those countries.

Many researchers have suggested that there are universal attributes
of transformational leadership that are endorsed and effective across all
cultures.[30] With regard to developing countries, for example, Woycke
analyzed the biographies of charismatic leaders in those countries and
concluded that they generally had characteristics that were consistent
with the four components identified by Bass and listed earlier.[31] Several
studies of leaders in India also concluded that successful leaders in that
country possessed the qualities commonly associated with transformational leaders.[32] However, Bass and others have also "accepted that though
the formulation of transformational leadership is in a relatively universal manner, a leader might need to act in different ways within differing

[28] Burns, J. 1978. *Leadership*, 20. New York, NY: Harper & Row.

[29] Bass, B.M. 1985. *Leadership and Performance Beyond Expectations.* New York,
NY: Free Press.

[30] See, e.g., Bass, B.M. 1997. "Does the Transactional-Transformational Leadership Paradigm Transcend Organizational and National Boundaries?" *American
Psychologist* 52, no. 2, pp. 130–39; and Den Hartog, D., R. House, P. Hanges,
S. Ruiz-Quintanilla, and P. Dorfman. 1999. "Culture Specific and Cross-cultur-
ally Generalizable Implicit Leadership Theories: Are Attributes of Charismatic/
transformational Leadership Universally Endorsed?" *Leadership Quarterly* 10,
no. 2, pp. 219–56.

[31] Woycke, J. 1990. "Managing Political Modernization: Charismatic Leadership in the Developing Countries." In *Management in Developing Countries*, eds.
A. Jaeger and R. Kanungo, 275–86. London: Routledge.

[32] See, e.g., Dayal, I. 1999. "Can Organizations Develop Leaders?" *A Study of
Effective Leaders*, 43–70. New Delhi: Mittal Publications.

cultural contexts."[33] For example, although transformational leadership is praised in Russia and other countries of Eastern Europe, two of the components—charisma and idealized consideration—have been found to be relatively less effective in influencing and improving the performance of followers.[34] Similarly, transformational leaders are cautioned to take the sociocultural environment into account when deciding on how best to communicate their vision to followers.[35]

Singh and Krishman summed up their review of the literature relative to the universality and culture contingency of attributes of transformational leadership by observing that "we see that even though the general definition of transformational leadership is applicable globally, its effective operationalization is culturally contingent."[36] They cautioned that leaders seeking to achieve transformational change in developing countries must be sensitive to "culture-specific complexities and nuances operating within their organizations"[37] and noted that perhaps the unsuccessful transfer of western management techniques, including transformational leadership systems, could be traced to a failure to identify, understand, and honor local ideologies and beliefs. Singh and Krishman went on to examine how effective transformational leadership was actually operationalized in India and found that whereas 44 percent of the responses they received from

---

[33] Singh, N., and V. Krishman. April-June 2005. "Towards Understanding Transformational Leadership in India: A Grounded Theory Approach." *The Journal of Business Perspective* 9, no. 2, pp. 5–17, 8. (citing Bass, B. 1997. "Does the Transactional-Transformational Leadership Paradigm Transcend Organizational and National Boundaries?" *American Psychologist* 52, no. 2, pp. 130–39).

[34] Ardichvili, A., and A. Gasparishvili. 2001. "Leadership Profiles of Managers in Post-Communist Countries: A Comparative Study." *Leadership & Organization Development Journal* 22, no. 2, pp. 62–69.

[35] Smith, P., and M. Peterson. 2002. "Cross-Cultural Leadership." In *The Blackwell Handbook of Cross-Cultural Management*, eds. M. Gannon and L. Newman, 217–35. Oxford: Blackwell Publishers Ltd.

[36] Singh, N., and V. Krishman. April-June 2005. "Towards Understanding Transformational Leadership in India: A Grounded Theory Approach." *The Journal of Business Perspective* 9, no. 2, pp. 5–17, 8.

[37] Id. at p. 8 (citing Singh, P., and A. Bhandarker. 1990. *Corporate Success and Transformational Leadership*, 344. New Delhi: Wiley Eastern.)

their survey group were consistent with the universal dimension of transformational leadership the remaining 56 percent of the responses were consistent with several culturally contingent "unique Indian dimensions" such as "nurturant" (20 percent), "personal touch" (13 percent), "expertise" (7 percent), "simple-living-high-thinking" (7 percent), "loyalty" (4 percent), "self-sacrifice" (3 percent), and "giving model of motivation" (2 percent). They concluded that a manager in India is more likely to emerge as a transformational leader if he or she "follows socially appreciable image (simple living) and encourages behaviors that are socially valued (selfless behavior, loyalty, culture of giving and personal touch)."[38]

Team-Oriented Leaders

The GLOBE researchers summarized their "team-oriented" leadership dimension as emphasizing "effective team building and implementation of a common purpose or goal among team members." Team-oriented leadership was quite popular among developing countries in the GLOBE study and clearly should resonate well in a cultural environment in which collectivism and harmonious personal interrelationships are valued. In fact, Aycan argued that the ideal leader in developing countries is a "team integrator" who is able to overcome certain sociocultural challenges existing in those countries to motivate employees to act as effective team members. However, Aycan also cautioned that the typical sociocultural profile in developing countries may at once promote and hinder effective teamwork. For example, she explains that whereas "[r]elationship-orientation may be perceived as an asset for teamwork ... the nature of relationships and in-group dynamics may hinder effectiveness."[39] One particular issue for managers in developing countries is putting together a team that has the appropriate mix of task-related knowledge and competencies. In a society where interpersonal harmony and "in-group" relationships are extremely important, team members may have difficulty working with

---

[38] Id. at p. 15.

[39] Aycan, Z. 2004. "Leadership and Teamwork in Developing Countries: Challenges and Opportunities." In *Online Readings in Psychology and Culture*, eds. W. Lonner, D. Dinnel, S. Hayes, and D. Sattler.

someone who is perceived to be from an "out-group" even if that person clearly has the skills needed for the team to achieve its stated business purpose. As Aycan observed: ". . . [t]eam members find it very difficult to work with someone who they 'don't know' or 'don't like' . . . [m]embers who have the potential to disturb in-group harmony are not wanted no matter how competent they may be."[40]

Another issue in organizing and managing teams in developing countries is the ability of the leader to maintain team cohesion, which is obviously necessary in order for the team to perform effectively and complete assigned tasks in a timely manner. Aycan suggests that teamwork requires egalitarian relationships and cautions that the status consciousness of team members and/or their suspicion of "out-group" members may lead to a failure to share information needed by other members of the team. Even among members of the same "in-group" there may be rivalries to obtain recognition and praise from the leader that undermine communication and collaboration. Ironically, too much team cohesion may undermine team performance also, as might be the case when group members become so tightly knit that they become reluctant to raise questions or create disagreements that might undermine team harmony even when it might be reasonable and appropriate to reconsider how a particular team activity is being conducted.[41]

Other potential impediments to effective teamwork in developing countries may appear in areas such as performance feedback, division of responsibility, and group discussions. With respect to performance feedback, the need to preserve harmony and not cause team members to lose "face" hampers efforts to provide negative feedback, even in situations where a team member is clearly not performing at the level required for the entire team to be effective. Criticism, particularly criticism delivered and received in the "wrong way," may cause the recipient to leave the team or remain and sabotage the efforts of other team members. The inability of team leaders in developing countries to establish procedures for evaluation performance and delivering feedback leads to another significant hurdle to effective team work: "social loafing" because there is

---

[40] Id.

[41] Id.

no consequence associated with doing a poor job. Social loafing may also occur because leaders do not clearly differentiate role assignments within the group and team members are unwilling to take the initiative on their own to define their jobs and/or assume additional responsibilities. Finally, Aycan notes that "[s]elf-representation is an important concern for people in developing countries" and suggests that this may cause members of teams in those countries to be uncomfortable about offering suggestions and criticisms in group meeting of team members, both of which are necessary for innovation and creativity, because of concerns about how they might be perceived and evaluated by others in the meeting.[42]

Aycan suggested that knowledge about potential sociocultural impediments to effective teamwork in developing countries can be used by team leaders in those countries to develop leadership styles and practices that can make them more effective "team integrators." Among the ideas offered by Aycan were the following[43]:

- Team leaders in developing countries must be skillful in both maintaining good interpersonal relations and setting high performance standards. Strong leadership is necessary for teams to flourish in developing countries because the sociocultural profile makes it unlikely that teams in those countries will be able to organize themselves and operate autonomously.
- Team leaders need to exercise caution and care when organizing teams to ensure that there is compatibility in terms of interpersonal relations; however, this does not mean that close friendship should be the only criterion for team membership, and leaders must also be sure that the group includes members with all the skills and knowledge required for the team to perform its business-related purpose.
- Team leaders need to be mindful of potential sources of insecurity and anxiety for team members and must proactively work to minimize "in-group" rivalries and establish and maintain group cohesiveness within the team such as by

---

[42] Id.

[43] Id.

sponsoring social activities which allow team members to get to know one another.

- Team leaders must seek to minimize "social loafing" by clearly defining roles and responsibilities for team members and should implement training programs for team members that teach them about important activities such as performance management and interteam collaboration and communications.
- Team leaders should take steps to improve the environment for conducting team meetings and soliciting feedback from team members on team performance.
- Team leaders should not only define roles and responsibilities for team members but also announce in advance the expected norms and values for the team so that all members understand in advance what is expected of them and the consequences associated with failure to perform in the expected manner.
- Team leaders should carefully orchestrate performance evaluations and rewards for good performance. Negative feedback regarding individual performance should be delivered privately and suggestions from the leader to improve team performance should be delivered in a manner that does not embarrass individual team members.
- Rewards should be based on group performance and distributed equitably among all team members.

Participative Leaders

Participative leaders seek to "involve others in making and implementing decisions" and participation is generally recognized around the world as making a positive contribution to effective leadership.[44] However, the results of the GLOBE survey confirmed the existence of significant differences among societies with respect to how leader efforts to involve

---

[44] Javidan, M., P. Dorfman, M. de Luque, and R. House. 2006. "In the Eye of the Beholder: Cross-Cultural Lessons in Leadership from Project GLOBE." *Academy of Management Perspectives* 20, no. 1, pp. 67–90, 73.

followers in decisions might be perceived. Not surprisingly, participative leadership received higher scores among industrialized societies with more individualistic cultural values and lower power distance; however, implementation of this style is likely to be more problematic in high power distance societies where followers are accustomed to differing to those in authority with respect to decisions and might even view attempts at including followers in decisions as a sign of weakness on the part of the leader. It may be that leaders in developing countries will be embracing participative leadership practices more vigorously in the future in response to external factors such as the need to expand communication channels within organizations in order to respond quickly to competitive conditions and the realization that "[e]mployees in developing countries—especially the young and well-educated generation—seek more participation in the decision-making process."[45]

Humane-Oriented Leaders

Humane-oriented leadership was perceived positively in all of the country clusters in the GLOBE survey; however, the scores in some of the clusters indicated that the effect of this style of leadership was essentially neutral whereas other clusters—Southern Asia, Sub-Saharan Africa, and Confucian Asia—reported that this style made a moderate contribution to effective leadership. Humane orientation "reflects supportive and considerate leadership but also includes compassion and generosity."[46] Although humane-oriented leadership has received relatively little attention in the leadership literature, scholars such as Winston and Ryan have argued that societies that view this style favorably may be fertile ground for use of techniques that have been associated with "servant leadership," which is based

---

[45] Aycan, Z. 2004. "Leadership and Teamwork in Developing Countries: Challenges and Opportunities." In *Online Readings in Psychology and Culture*, eds. W. Lonner, D. Dinnel, S. Hayes, and D. Sattler. http://ac.wwu.edu/~culture/readings.htm

[46] Javidan, M., P. Dorfman, M. de Luque, and R. House. 2006. "In the Eye of the Beholder: Cross-Cultural Lessons in Leadership from Project GLOBE." *Academy of Management Perspectives* 20, no. 1, pp. 67–90, 73.

on the notion that leaders act for altruistic rather than self-serving reasons and seek to serve their followers and assist them in achieving their vision as opposed to engaging in "command-control" leadership behaviors.[47] Winston and Ryan explained that elements of GLOBE's humane orientation construct may be found in traditional religious teachings that have their roots in Africa (Ubuntu, Harambee), East Asia (Taoist, Confucianism), the Mediterranean area (Judaism), and India (Hindu). Kumuyi also discussed the utility of "servant leadership" in Africa and observed that "what Africa needs for its redemption is servant leadership instead of the self-serving governance that the continent is famed for."[48] He argued that African leaders, particularly in the political arena, should study the principles of servant leadership in order to learn how to lead by seeking to "serve and help."[49]

Perspectives on Leadership from Development Leaders in Developing Countries

Jeffrey Yergler, a student and teacher of leadership development, identified 10 interesting and compelling leadership prospective among a group of development leaders, social reformers, and social entrepreneurs from 12 developing nations in Asia:

1. *Humility*: The primary concerns of the development leaders were not themselves or their development agendas, but rather the

---

[47] Winston, B., and B. Ryan. 2008. "Servant Leadership as a Humane Orientation: Using the GLOBE Study Construct of Humane Orientation to Show that Servant Leadership is More Global than Western." *International Journal of Leadership Studies* 3, no. 2, pp. 212–22, 213. For further discussion of "servant leadership," see "Leadership Styles" prepared and distributed by the Sustainable Entrepreneurship Project (www.seproject.org).

[48] McIntosh, T., and J. Irving. 2010. "Evaluating the Instrumento de Contribución al Liderazgo de Siervo (ICLS) for Reliability in Latin America." *Journal of Virtues and Leadership* 1, no. 1, pp. 30–49, 33. (citing Kumuyi, W. June 2007. "The Case for Servant Leadership." *New Africa*, pp. 18–19.)

[49] Id.

well-being of those they worked with and those with whom they served. Their perspective and approach embodied the principles of servant leadership.

2. *Get Your Hands Dirty*: The development leaders worked in the trenches within their communities, making sure that they were involved, connected, participating, collaborating, and deeply integrated in the work of their organization. They avoided hierarchies or any other barriers to personal engagement in difficult issues and delegated and empowered others.

3. *Courage and Risk Taking*: The development leaders had no concern for self-preservation and were fully aware of the challenges and issues they need to address from individuals or groups who oppose their work and want them to fail.

4. *Taking the Long View*: The development leaders were committed and patient and took a long-term view that acknowledged and accepted that progress would be measured person by person, brick by brick, initiative by initiative, and project by project. Their current work was all that mattered and was not a stepping stone to something "more important."

5. *Professional Development and Talent Management*: The development leaders were eager to receive training on leading, leadership, and talent management and sought sustainable processes and tools to not only support their own leadership learning but also develop the skills of those serving with them in their organizations.

6. *Collaboration and Partnerships*: The development leaders understood that collaborations and partnerships were essential to their impact on their communities and that they needed to be open to learning and exploring with others regarding leadership and management, overcoming obstacles, and making connections.

7. *Kindness and Generosity*: The development leaders understood the importance of kindness, consideration, and generosity and the value of the opportunities provided by their roles to grow develop, interact, and learn.

8. *It's about the Story*: The development leaders understood that whereas experience and education were important to their ability

to perform their roles, in order to be effective they needed to be able to weave their knowledge through narratives that provided multiple perspectives and insights that impacted the lives of those whom they were trying to help.

9. *Fidelity and Loyalty to Those Served by the Mission*: The development leaders had a fierce commitment and resolve to their mission and especially those who are served/impacted through the mission. All of the time, resources, energy, and resolve of the development leaders were consistently directed toward their work.

10. *Resilience and Hope*: The multitude of challenges, points of resistance, and setbacks for development leaders makes it imperative that they be resilient human beings and people who are capable to remaining hopeful about the progress of their mission in the face of resistance, risks, and potential danger.

Source: Yergler, J. June 13, 2017. "What Leaders from Developing Nations Can Teach the West about Leadership: 10 Perspectives." https://linkedin.com/pulse/what-leaders-from-developing-nations-can-teach-west-yergler-ph-d-?trk=v-feed&lipi=urn%3Ali%3Apage%3Ad_flagship3_feed%3Bf7pnqA3AiD3jYHRLis5AaA%3D%3D

Research on Leadership Styles in Developing Countries

Although not yet as robust as the research work conducted on leadership styles and behaviors in developed countries there has been an increasing interest in studying leadership in developing countries. In general, the most commonly identified leadership style in developing countries has been paternalism and a distinction has often been drawn between "authoritative" and "benevolent" paternalism. As described by Pasa et al., authoritative paternalism includes "emphasis on duty and lacks since generosity on the part of the superior" whereas benevolent paternalism "emphasizes the subordinate's loyalty and the superior's generous concern for that subordinate."[50] Studies conducted on leadership in Korea and Turkey both led to conclusions that authoritative paternalism was prevalent in those countries.[51] Research conducted on Japanese leadership during a period when that country was still "developing" pointed to a mix of performance- and maintenance-oriented behaviors as being most effective.[52] Sinha singled out "nurturant task leadership" as being effective in India.[53] Finally, Kanungo and Mendonca argued that perhaps charismatic leadership might be appropriate for progress in developing countries because charismatic leaders are likely to be more proactive in initiating changes needed in those countries for economic and social development to proceed.[54]

---

[50] Pasa, S., H. Kabasakal, and M. Bodur. 2001. "Society, Organisations and Leadership in Turkey." *Applied Psychology: An International Review* 50, no. 4, pp. 559–89, 566. They explained further that "[p]aternalism includes elements of both autocratic and nurturant behaviors where the leader acts like a father to the followers" (citing Kabasakal, H., and M. Bodur. 1998. *Leadership, Values and Institutions: The Case of Turkey.* Bogazici University Research Papers, Istanbul).

[51] See Kim, U. 1994. "Significance of Paternalism and Communalism in the Occupational Welfare System of Korean firms: A National Survey." In *Individualism and Collectivism: Theory, Method and Applications* (*Cross-Cultural Research and Methodology, No. 18*), eds. U. Kim, J. Triandis, C. Kagitcibasi, S. Choi, and G. Yoon, 251–66. Thousand Oaks, CA: Sage; and Dilber, M. 1967. *Management in the Turkish Private Sector Industry.* Ann Arbor, MI: University Microfilms, Inc.

[52] Misumi, J., and M. Peterson. June 1985. "The Performance-Maintenance (PM) Theory of Leadership: Revised of a Japanese Research Program." *Administrative Science Quarterly*, pp. 198–223.

[53] Sinha, J. 1990. "A Model of Effective Leadership Styles in India." In *Management in Developing Countries*, eds. A. Jaeger and R. Kanungo. London: Routledge.

[54] Kanungo, R., and M. Mendonca. 1996. "Cultural Contingencies and Leadership in Developing Countries." *Sociology of Organizations* 14, pp. 263–95.

About the Author

Dr. Alan S. Gutterman is the founding director of the Sustainable Entrepreneurship Project (www.seproject.org). In addition, Alan's prolific output of practical guidance and tools for legal and financial professionals, managers, entrepreneurs, and investors has made him one of the best-selling individual authors in the global legal publishing marketplace. His cornerstone work, *Business Transactions Solution*, is on online-only product available and featured on Thomson Reuters' Westlaw, the world's largest legal content platform, which includes almost 200 book-length modules covering the entire life cycle of a business. Alan has also authored or edited over 70 books on sustainable entrepreneurship, management, business law and transactions, international law business and technology management for a number of publishers including Thomson Reuters, Kluwer, Aspatore, Oxford, Quorum, ABA Press, Aspen, Sweet & Maxwell, Euromoney, Business Expert Press, Harvard Business Publishing, CCH, and BNA. Alan has over three decades of experience as a partner and senior counsel with internationally recognized law firms counseling small and large business enterprises in the areas of general corporate and securities matters, venture capital, mergers and acquisitions, international law and transactions, strategic business alliances, technology transfers and intellectual property, and has also held senior management positions with several technology-based businesses including service as the chief legal officer of a leading international distributor of IT products headquartered in Silicon Valley and as the chief operating officer of an emerging broadband media company. He has been an adjunct faculty member at several colleges and universities, including Boalt Hall, Golden Gate University, Hastings College of Law, Santa Clara University, and the University of San Francisco, teaching classes on a diverse range of topics including corporate finance, venture capital, corporate law, Japanese business law and law and economic development, He received his AB, MBA, and JD from the University of California at Berkeley, a DBA from Golden Gate University, and a PhD from the University of Cambridge. For more information about Alan and his activities, please contact him directly at alangutterman@gmail.com, follow him on LinkedIn (https://www.linkedin.com/in/alangutterman/) and visit his website at alangutterman.com, which includes an extensive collection of links to his books and other publications and resource materials for students and practitioners of sustainable entrepreneurship.

Index

OTHER TITLES IN THE HUMAN RESOURCE MANAGEMENT AND ORGANIZATIONAL BEHAVIOR COLLECTION

- *Conflict First Aid: How to Stop Personality Clashes and Disputes from Damaging You or Your Organization* by Nancy Radford
- *How to Manage Your Career: The Power of Mindset in Fostering Success* by Kelly Swingler
- *Deconstructing Management Maxims, Volume I: A Critical Examination of Conventional Business Wisdom* by Kevin Wayne
- *Deconstructing Management Maxims, Volume II: A Critical Examination of Conventional Business Wisdom* by Kevin Wayne
- *The Real Me: Find and Express Your Authentic Self* by Mark Eyre
- *Across the Spectrum: What Color Are You?* by Stephen Elkins-Jarrett
- *The Human Resource Professional's Guide to Change Management: Practical Tools and Techniques to Enact Meaningful and Lasting Organizational Change* by Melanie J. Peacock
- *Tough Calls: How to Move Beyond Indecision and Good Intentions* by Linda D. Henman
- *The 360 Degree CEO: Generating Profits While Leading and Living with Passion and Principles* by Lorraine A. Moore
- *The Concise Coaching Handbook: How to Coach Yourself and Others to Get Business Results* by Elizabeth Dickinson

Announcing the Business Expert Press Digital Library

Concise e-books business students need for classroom and research

This book can also be purchased in an e-book collection by your library as

- a one-time purchase,
- that is owned forever,
- allows for simultaneous readers,
- has no restrictions on printing, and
- can be downloaded as PDFs from within the library community.

Our digital library collections are a great solution to beat the rising cost of textbooks. E-books can be loaded into their course management systems or onto students' e-book readers.
The **Business Expert Press** digital libraries are very affordable, with no obligation to buy in future years. For more information, please visit **www.businessexpertpress.com/librarians**. To set up a trial in the United States, please email **sales@businessexpertpress.com**.